You Are Not Alone

Your Guide for When Divorce is On Your Doorstep

Shell Sawyer, CDFA®

ISBN Paperback: 979-8-9917946-0-2

Cover Design by Elizabeth B. Hill and Shell Sawyer

Cover Image Credit: Anne-Marie Libotte from Getty Images

Contents

Dedication

This book is dedicated to ...

My Dad.
Thank you for your love and guidance.
You have made me into the person I am today.
I miss you and I hope I make you proud.

My wonderful daughter.
Thank you for cheering me on and for your continuous support.
You bring love and laughter to my heart.
I love our chats and our time together.
I love being your mom.

My Scott (and the New Zoo Review).
Thank you for bringing light to my days and nights.
Your patience and kindness made this book and my business possible.
Thank you for always listening and giving me valuable advice.

Symbolism of Doors

A door holds a deep symbolic meaning that extends beyond its physical presence. It represents the boundary between the known and the unknown, the familiar and unfamiliar. A door can represent a shift of our attention from closed doors to the opportunities that lie ahead. A closed door symbolizes the past, while an open door looks toward the future. It serves as a reminder to embrace change and new beginnings, as they offer the potential for growth and fulfillment.

Foreword

Overwhelm. Shame. Guilt. Fear. These are just some of the many emotions my psychotherapy clients present with when they are sitting across from me contemplating divorce.

I know a thing or two about divorce. Not only have I gone through my own divorce, but I have dedicated my career as a psychotherapist and divorce recovery coach to helping clients all along the divorce continuum.

What I know for sure is that making the decision to divorce is quite possibly one of the hardest decisions you'll ever make ... but it can also be one of the best things that ever happens to you.

In my private practice, when my clients are contemplating walking through the door of divorce, they often ask me, "How do I know if I'm making the right decision?" ... "How will I afford to live on my own?" ... "Should I just suck it up and try harder?" ... "How will my kids handle a divorce?" ... "If I get divorced, will I be alone forever?"

Do any of these sound familiar?

I support clients in finding clarity on their decision to stay married or proceed with a divorce. I offer guidance, support, encouragement, and hope. To help them "tackle" the overwhelm that is almost always associated with divorce, I recommend this book.

I met Shell Sawyer several years ago through a local networking group. We instantly connected before learning that we both have businesses supporting clients who are contemplating or going through a divorce. As a Certified Divorce Financial Analyst®, mediator, and Certified Divorce Coach®, Shell became my go-to referral source for clients who had questions about finances as they relate to divorce, as well as questions about the divorce process. My clients would report back to me after consulting with Shell that she was kind, compassionate, knowledgeable, and non-judgmental. They reported feeling safe and understood by her.

In this book, Shell not only shares her own lived experience with divorce, but she shares her knowledge and expertise as a divorce professional. Using door symbolism and metaphors, she provides her reader with powerful reflection points, things to consider when walking through the doorway to divorce, as well as helpful tips, checklists, and templates.

You Are Not Alone: Your Guide for When Divorce is on Your Doorstep is a must-have guide for anyone who is contemplating divorce. Reading this book will give you the knowledge to confidently move forward with less fear and more hope.

Making the decision to divorce is life-changing. It takes courage and it takes strength. But, on the other side of that door, an amazing life is just waiting for you to create it.

Lucinda Testo
Owner of Unlimited You
Psychotherapist & Divorce Recovery Coach

Introduction

LESSONS FROM CLOSED DOORS

No one ever thinks that when they get married, they will get divorced.

No one!

Well, except me.

That was probably my insecurities talking.

I remember feeling the day before my wedding, "This may not be forever, but I am going to enjoy it while it lasts." I may have even muttered it out loud. I cannot remember who I muttered it to, but I am sure their mouth was agape, and they had no response. Why would they? That is not what you would expect from someone getting married *TOMORROW*.

In November 2015, during a party at a friend's house, my spouse unexpectedly left agitated, expressing his intention of going home and leaving me there to fend for myself. However, after being dropped off by my friends, I discovered he was nowhere to be found. This departure was particularly unusual as it was the first time he had ever behaved in such a manner.

Following a prolonged silence, I persuaded him to dedicate effort to improving our marriage. I meticulously pointed out all the compelling reasons why it was worth the effort to save our relationship. He reluctantly agreed but wasn't interested in couples therapy, date nights, or anything else I could throw at him. So, from that point on, I tried to mentally prepare myself for the "D" word to rear its ugly head again.

I wanted to shield myself from the hurt that I knew could come back at any time. I donned metaphorical armor and braced myself, preparing for incoming fire. The armor must have been flawed because the arrows pierced through, leaving me wounded.

Mate for Life

We all hope that when we find "the one," we will spend the rest of our lives with them. We envision our lives together and dream about our future, the family we will have, the destinations we will explore, and the life we will build. We form strong bonds together and create many memories with our spouses. We share responsibilities to form a caring and nurturing home.

As a child, my family lived in a small home with one bathroom for four people. My dad was a friendly, kind soul with a smile that went on for days. I looked up to him; he was my hero. What I particularly remember about his demeanor is that he was always joyful and positive, even when talking to himself in the bathroom. He spoke, hummed, and sang in the bathroom while showering and shaving, preparing himself for the day ahead. He was the hardest worker I knew; he held multiple jobs as a machinist while sometimes picking up shifts at a local liquor store in the evening and on weekends. He should have been an accountant, as he had a keen eye for numbers. I got my love of numbers and work ethic from him.

When he talked to himself in the bathroom, I would ask, "Dad, who are you talking to?" I was young, maybe four or five.

He would say, "Harvey!"

Dad was a big James Stewart fan and loved all comedians, especially Robin Williams. He made me appreciate a good laugh and taught me not to take myself so seriously.

"Who is Harvey, Dad?" I asked.

"He is a cross between a penguin and a rabbit," he replied. Of course he is. My dad loved penguins, which was appropriate because living in a rookery would have suited him well.

My dad was loyal.

My dad was dedicated.

My dad was a family man.

My dad was a Proper Penguin.

Penguins are usually associated with monogamy but are fascinating relationship experts. They form lasting partnerships, and their parents actively raise their fuzzy little chicks together.

Birdfact.com, a website dedicated to birdwatching worldwide, states that partner fidelity in certain penguin species can be as high as 89%.[1]

- Raising a chick in a harsh environment takes TWO COMMITTED partner penguins.

- A penguin's home (their nest) binds a pair together.

- Penguins that use the same nest site can exhibit high mate fidelity.

- Most penguins will pair up with the same partner each year if they have successfully raised chicks in the last season.

Those dapper tuxedo-clad birds are intelligent creatures from which we can learn much about relationships. All most of us ever ask for is to be loved like a penguin.

This book is not just a story about surviving a divorce but also about partnership, finding lessons and opportunities from closed doors, and the power of penguins.

Resilience Forged in Broken Crayons

From the outside, my childhood home must have looked picture-perfect. We lived in a quintessential quiet town in a suburb of Connecti-

---

1. https://birdfact.com/articles/do-penguins-mate-for-life

cut—where everyone knows each other, you attend Friday night football games under the lights, and you spend the weekend keeping up with the Joneses.

At a recent family party, one of my cousins noted how she envied my upbringing. I was always envious of HER! She has a strong bond with her three siblings, who care deeply for one another. While my childhood was certainly comfortable and idyllic from the outside, with a lovely home, a pool in the backyard, and many friends, I had a secret that I had kept hidden from the world.

That story took me a long time to process, let alone even discuss, but here I am, sharing it with the world because I know there are others, just like me, who need me to release the truth. My truth is, as a young child, a close family member sexually abused me. Someone that I trusted.

But it wasn't enough that this happened; what truly impacted me was when I brought it up to someone I loved and trusted, even though I was threatened not to, they brushed it under the rug. I was told not to discuss it further or mention it to anyone else. In my young eyes, I took that chance, mustering up the courage and strength to tell someone what was happening to me. My cry for help fell on deaf ears. Oh, the tears and disappointment that I felt. I asked for help and did not receive any in return, and my voice was not heard by the people who mattered most.

In the dreams that recur often, I'm in situations where I desperately attempt to scream, but to my dismay, no sound escapes my lips. It's a frustrating experience that leaves me feeling powerless and unsettled. In other parts of the dreams, I have an urgent need to dial a phone number, but as I scramble to input the digits, some are missing, or the call simply won't go through, leaving me with a sense of disconnection and frustration. Despite the distress these dreams bring, I've grasped their significance.

Looking for Love in all the Wrong Places

After many years of therapy, I understand now that I have abandonment issues that stem from my feeling of being alone and that I could not rely on my loved ones to support or take care of me. Someone said, "Being excessively independent can result from constantly being let down and hurt, leading to a defense mechanism to protect oneself from future disappointment." I felt this in my soul. I was looking for love in all the wrong places, hoping to find someone who could care for me and provide me with a sense of security.

My first husband left me in much debt. Even before we married, I felt some shady things were brewing. I was questioning whether or not I should marry him, but I felt pressured to make everyone happy and continue with the wedding we planned. The invitations were out, the deposits were made, and the bridal showers were given. You know, that is my MO—a people pleaser. Unfortunately, this decision disappointed ME the most and made me feel unworthy and unlovable. It took me a long time to forgive myself for this mistake. By the time I decided to leave, I just wanted out! So, I forfeited some things, like equity in our home, that could have, at the very least, given me enough money to get me going in my next chapter. Instead, I left financially devastated, with no money in my pocket and debt that I had to conquer.

After this experience, I learned a valuable lesson. I now understand the importance of getting what you deserve in divorce. I mastered the art of financial management, learned how to conquer my cash flow, and found tried and true methods to pay off my debt. Today, I use my experience to help others who may be going through similar situations. So, there is no judgment here, as I have walked in your shoes. I'll share my proven methods to overcome financial difficulties. If I could do it, you can too!

My missteps in the love department may explain why I love dogs so much! Dogs don't care if you are pretty, intelligent, awkward, or emotional. They don't even mind whether or not you are financially secure, although they would like you to have enough money to buy an occasional treat or chew toy. They love you regardless of your personality or upbringing. They only want you to love them and give them food and treats. They will always protect you and, most importantly, never leave you! That is unconditional love! And let's face it; there are times when you need the warmth and compassion of a dog to recover from interactions with other humans, especially during a divorce. I don't know what I would do without them sometimes.

Despite my low self-esteem, I still had hope (and a dog). Through all that had happened and all the doors that had closed on me, I saw this as an opportunity to find an open door, an open door for love. That's when I met the father of my daughter.

They say people come into your life for a reason, a season, or a lifetime. I believe he came to me for a reason. Not only did he bring people into my life who showed me love, but he also built up my self-esteem. As I mentioned at the beginning of my story, I did not go into this marriage lightly. I went in with trepidation and strolled forward with baby steps, thinking, "Eventually, the other shoe will drop."

We had fun together, we laughed, we had similar upbringings, my dog liked him, and we both liked each other's families. We built a wonderful life. I adored his family; they became mine. They welcomed me in with open arms and embraced my shattered soul. I finally knew what it was like to be loved. We shared holidays and family time. His mom became my best friend, and we talked on the phone every day. I respected her and enjoyed our friendship. His dad embraced me like his own daughter. This man was the strongest man I knew; he had been through many medical issues but always came out on top.

His family welcomed my parents into their lives, too. They were our rocks when my dad was diagnosed with Alzheimer's. We could always count on them for just about anything. In the past, I never wanted to ask anyone for help or rely on anyone else, as I thought they would always let me down. But this felt good. I learned to trust again.

Then I was crushed!

This time was different than what I felt before. This was Pain (with a capital "P"). I felt like my body was going to burst. I always knew how to manage my issues; if you can call it that (I would shove them down and not think about them).

Have you ever heard the saying "reality is an acquired taste"? If you avoid reality altogether, you don't have to face it. Or, if you always think the worst will happen and then it doesn't, you won't be disappointed.

This time, my guard was down. I had learned to trust. I cried and bellowed. I probably sounded like one of those coyotes you hear in the dead of night, capturing their prey on the foothills of death. You may have heard me! I was now fighting for survival.

Was I destined to walk alone? Or at least walk alongside a dog; this time, two. Rudolf (Rudy) and Snowball (Snowy). At the time of my writing, Rudy and Snowy have unfortunately crossed the rainbow bridge.

I have a soul mate now, Cypress.

All I could think about was all that I was losing.
His family had become mine.
My daughter was enjoying her life.
I had a community I loved.
Friends that I cherished.
My church that warmed my soul.
A neighborhood where we all belonged.
The dreams we had envisioned shattered.
My heart was truly breaking.

You Are Not Alone

At the age of 47, the prospect of being alone again was a frightening thought for me. I had been in this situation before and managed to overcome it by relying on my strength and resilience. However, this time, it felt worse. My father had passed away, and my mother was experiencing health issues of her own, so I could not depend on them for support. Doors had opened for me, and I had become accustomed to being loved and accepted by others. I didn't want to go back to closed doors, feeling insecure and vulnerable again. I was my own worst enemy, and I was afraid of falling back into negative thought patterns that held me back. This fear is not external; it is rooted in my mind and thoughts, which can sometimes be my biggest obstacle.

I want to express my gratitude for everything I was able to enjoy. During that time, I felt happy and fortunate to have a life that some people can only dream of, even if it was shorter than I had hoped. The truth of the matter is that I never wanted that to end. I have traveled a long road and have learned to accept it. I still face some challenges, but they are different and consume less of my energy. They say time heals all wounds, which I challenge; I am not sure it was time, but rather the opportunity to process my pain and alter my perception. Because of this, I believe you must use your time well and do some soul-searching with the time you have to heal.

I'm sharing this with you because you may be experiencing similar emotions. Your story might differ, but I hope my words comfort you and let you know you're not alone.

Stars Emerge from Night's Embrace

It might be challenging to imagine when you are on the steps of divorce, but if you look hard enough—it's there—you can see the light peeking through the trees. Can you see it? Close your eyes and envision the most beautiful of sights. Do you see the open door ahead? The path forward may feel a little rocky, and the steps may not be sturdy, but the light will blind you once you reach the open door and walk through it.

The great thing about all this is that now I have a sense of appreciation for all that has happened! When you have been through some of the things I have been through—abuse, parents with health issues, death, and divorce—it all sits with you. It's like a trophy for a race you did not want to participate in. After the race, it is not at the top of your mind, and you barely notice the trophy anymore, sitting on the proverbial shelf, but it is there.

A feeling of gratefulness remains, knowing that you can help others walk through a similar situation. If someone approaches me who has a parent with Alzheimer's or is in a nursing home, I can provide guidance and suggestions. I can be a board member for the Interval House, which works to end intimate partner violence. And the best thing that has come out of this is that I started a business to help others walk down the path of divorce. I can help a fearful soul not only survive divorce but thrive in their next chapter.

How to Use This Book

Consider this book a guide and a journal, providing comfort and a pathway forward when divorce is on your doorstep. I have included questions throughout for you to reflect on. When you encounter the questions, I invite you to pause momentarily and step through the doorway of your thoughts. Let each question be a key that unlocks new rooms within your mind, calling you to explore and reflect. There is a section in the back for you to use for journaling if you so desire. Under the chapter "Workbook" you will find a QR code to access a workbook with helpful templates and checklists.

While writing this book, I created a survey and conducted follow-up interviews with friends and colleagues who have experienced divorce. This information is sprinkled throughout. I am thankful that these helpful souls took the time to candidly share their thoughts, trials, tribulations, and triumphs so I could share them with you. My hope is their words may comfort you on your journey.

The chapters revolve around a common theme. Please skip to any section that interests you or read the whole thing in its entirety—the choice is yours.

You are not alone.

"When people show you who they are,

believe them the first time."

– Maya Angelou

I

Living With Your Hurt

DOORS SWING OPEN WHEN DESTINY KNOCKS

M aybe, just maybe, how you thought your life was "supposed" to be was not how it was meant to be at all. Perhaps your destiny is written differently than you imagined. I am confident that sometimes things go wrong so we can find what is right.

I am sure the nearly 700,000 couples that get divorced in the U.S. every year, a figure *Forbes Advisor* reported in their article "Revealing Divorce Statistics in 2024," can tell you a story or two about their divorce.[1] Most may even be able to share something positive that came out of their circumstances, even if it was only that they are stronger because of it.

We are so sure that we will not be a statistic and that our relationship has the staying power that we spend thousands of dollars on our wedding to celebrate our strong bond. We plan and prepare for months, sometimes even years, to make everything perfect.

We work hard to improve our skills and become viable employees. I don't think I am saying anything out of line here, but most people don't make the same effort with their marriages. Do you know anyone who

---

1.

https://www.forbes.com/advisor/legal/divorce/divorce-statistics/#:~:text=In%202022%2 C%20a%20total%20of%20673%2C989%20divorces%20and,the%20U.S.%20marriage%20 rate%206.2%20per%201%2C000%20people .

has taken a course to improve their relationship skills? We can't expect a healthy relationship without effort, yet most of us do.

Consequently, when issues arise in our relationship, we may choose denial and distraction to keep those problems unresolved and disregard the necessary steps for improvement.

Maybe you feel like something is off and not quite right, but you can't put your finger on it. To go along with the saying, "If it is not broke, don't fix it," maybe it just needs a little adjusting. Has it been a while since those kisses felt like a genuine connection? Yup, I get it; you're exhausted, and some days, you want to throw your hands up. Perhaps you are wondering what this is all for.

Yes, it takes some effort to throw in the towel, but you still don't know if you should ride it out to see what happens and if things will get better. Do you feel stuck between a rock and a hard place?

I know it is hard when you meet someone and your heart feels they're "The One," only to realize that they aren't who you thought they were at all. Some days, life is good, and you feel happy, like you can continue this trip around the sun together; other days, throwing in the towel seems like the answer.

Two themes emerged in my survey responses. First, the majority felt they wished they had gotten divorced sooner. Second, they didn't regret getting divorced at all.

Divorce rates peak between the third and seventh year of marriage. Couples who divorce after nine years or more often cite more severe issues, such as infidelity and lack of intimacy. And even though every marriage is unique, experts say one or more of these factors are usually to blame in every divorce. I wanted to share these themes with you to meet you where you are right now, with hopes that one or more of these themes might resonate. There are probably many other reasons people divorce, but I tried to capture the most common areas.

Here they are, in no particular order.

Monetary Barriers

A survey conducted by the Pew Research Center and published in early 2023 found that women earn 82 cents for every dollar men earn. This is a significant improvement from 1982 when women earned only 65 cents for every dollar earned by men. Divorce is already an expensive process, but it is even more financially burdensome for women. Despite these financial challenges, women tend to fare better immediately after divorce and thrive after it. So, don't let this hold you back.

One of my colleagues and friends said that she was so scared of all the debt they had accumulated that she felt stuck in her marriage and feared there was no way out. Eventually, she built up her strength and made that first step forward. I asked her, "Was it hard?" the answer was, "*Yes!*" Of course, it was hard, but she figured it all out and is in a good place now. We do hard things, girl! Her only regret is that she didn't do it sooner. She answered, "*I'd pick divorce a million times over!*"

If your spouse's healthcare plan currently covers you, you may lose coverage and need to get your own in some states. Fortunately, thanks to the Affordable Care Act, we now have multiple options and easier access to healthcare coverage. Don't let your lack of insurance coverage keep you in an unhealthy relationship. You can consider getting healthcare coverage through your employer. If that's not an option, you can check with your state's health insurance marketplace for affordable, income-based plans.

Every marriage has a different way of managing finances. The key to all of it is communication. If one spouse holds the financial reins without input from the other, trouble could be looming.

I have witnessed a few clients living with a spouse who manages and controls the finances. My client, who we'll call Rhonda, has a husband who gave her a weekly allowance but didn't allow her to access invoices or statements. The tax documents required her signature at tax time, but she didn't even know what she was signing her name to.

It is no surprise that money may be challenging for couples to talk about. We are often taught not to talk about money as we grow up, and we learn behaviors about our finances. "Money, you see, isn't just about bills and bank accounts. It's about power, control, security, and sometimes, it's even about love," says Laura Wasser, relationship expert and chief of divorce evolution at Divorce.com.

It is acceptable for one spouse to take the lead with your finances, paying the bills, or investing, but it is in your relationship's best interest for all parties to be aware of and included in the decision-making. When sharing financial resources, reckless spending, refusal to budget, and hidden debts can be severe issues. If concerns are ignored and the family's safety is at risk, trust in the relationship is undermined. Communication and joint decision-making may prevent money problems from becoming a deal-breaker in marriage.

All parties should stay active in household finances, and if you are not, now is an excellent time to start. Otherwise, you may be in for surprises if divorce knocks on your door before you are ready. Being involved also means that if there ever comes a time when you need to take on the family finances yourself, you will know what to do.

It may be a red flag if you communicate your financial concerns openly with your spouse and no action is taken to rectify them.

If there is concern your spouse is potentially hiding assets or has suspicious methods, please seek help from an attorney so they can take steps to help you find those assets. If you're experiencing financial difficulties, you know it can be challenging, but that doesn't mean you're out of options.

Don't let feeling financially unstable stop you from leaving your marriage.

Here are some ideas to consider if you are experiencing financial insecurity:

1. **<u>Seek alternative legal advice</u>** – There is no doubt that attorney fees are the most significant expense in your divorce. However, there are some alternatives to research, such as looking for a Legal Aid Center in your area. Legal Aid aims to provide civil legal aid to low-income families nationwide. You can search for pro bono lawyers online, ask your local courthouse, or on the American Bar Association website.

2. **<u>Consider mediation</u>** – Mediation is a lower-cost alternative to obtaining a divorce. A mediator helps you determine the details of your divorce. They facilitate conversations about splitting assets, deciding childcare agreements, and who takes on what debt from a marriage. The mediator will draw up a contract for both parties to sign when everything is accounted for. The process is impartial, voluntary, and confidential, and most importantly, it allows the parties involved to make the final decisions rather than attorneys or judges.

3. **<u>Reach out for help</u>** – Not everyone has friends or family members who can help them financially. However, there are other ways that they can lend a hand, such as by helping you find deals on furniture for your new apartment, providing childcare while you attend divorce sessions, assisting with your move, and more. It's a good idea to check with charitable organizations, religious groups, or local buy-nothing groups on Facebook before you shop for things to set up your new home.

4. **<u>Keep things amicable</u>** - Keeping things civil is another way to keep divorce costs low. This approach allows you to separate amicably and save money by paying less to lawyers and avoiding divorce courts. It also helps to minimize animosity between you and your spouse. Hatred can lead to spiteful actions, and you

don't want your spouse to try to ask for more in court due to any ill feelings.

5. **<u>Create a budget</u>** - Learning how to manage your money can be overwhelming, especially if you weren't the partner who handled finances. But don't let that discourage you from setting yourself up for success. There are plenty of budgeting apps available that you could use to track your spending and avoid wasting money. Use them to see what you're spending your money on. You could cut back if you notice that your spending is inflated in one area or another. The goal when budgeting is to create a balanced spending plan that covers all your expenses and leaves you with money left to save.

If you think you're on the doorstep of divorce, start putting a plan into place and organize your finances to be better prepared when you discuss it with your spouse.

Navigating the Revolving Door of a Critical Spouse

Perhaps you feel like your spouse is constantly criticizing or undervaluing you. Maybe they laugh at your expense and don't take it seriously when you express your discomfort, or perhaps they focus more on your mistakes than your accomplishments. This conduct can be a form of manipulation or what is known as "Gaslighting." The term comes from the 1938 play "Gaslight" by Patrick Hamilton[2], in which a husband tries to convince his wife that she's losing her mind to distract her from his criminal behavior.

Gaslighting is said to aim at controlling you and damaging your self-esteem and self-worth. When you attempt to address it with the person responsible, perhaps they don't apologize for doing anything wrong; instead, they blame you for reacting the way you did. This "blame-speak"

---

2. https://en.wikipedia.org/wiki/Gas_Light

Bill Edy[3] refers to, is a skillful deflection intended to evade accountability and divert attention from the real issues.

At first, they were charming and charismatic, but now you wonder where that lovely person went. Sounds all too familiar, doesn't it?

This behavior can be puzzling. Your partner may even portray themselves as the victim rather than the perpetrator. It can feel like looking through a carnival mirror where all images are altered. It leaves people second-guessing their own experiences, doubting their memories, and questioning their sanity.

I frequently hear about this issue from my clients. They confide in me about their experiences, which bring them sadness at first but later lead to confusion and sometimes even anger. I can understand how difficult this must be for them. And regardless of the circumstances that brought them to this point, it is manipulation and emotional abuse. The words their spouse uses to degrade and instill fear tactics hold immense power and leave emotional scars that can be just as damaging as the physical ones.

Pay attention to these signs, as they may indicate that you are in a toxic love relationship:

- You want your spouse to stop treating you this way and return to how things were.

- You justify their behavior to your friends and family.

- Your relationship causes you more pain than joy.

- You stay in the relationship, hoping that things will improve.

- Your partner is putting little to no effort into the relationship.

---

3. https://highconflictinstitute.com/high-conflict-strategies/excerpt-reacting-to-blamespeak/

- Your partner may struggle with showing empathy and under-standing.

- Your partner is causing you emotional, physical, or financial harm.

- Your relationship is preventing both of you from progressing.

When communicating with a toxic partner, it's crucial to avoid using hurtful labels like "narcissist" or "gaslighter" as it can escalate the conflict. No one wants to be labeled as a narcissist, especially if they display these traits.

It may initially appear like a difference of opinion or occurrence, but a gaslighter intentionally makes the recipient second guess their reality. They may be so convincing that the recipient might even believe their accusations. I emphasize to my clients that hurtful words hold less power and meaning if you don't give them the ability to affect you.

Becoming more self-aware is one of the most effective ways to combat this. As you learn more about yourself, you'll better recognize gaslighting and stand up against those inaccurate statements. Don't let them take your power.

Coercive control is a profoundly distressing form of manipulation and abuse. It occurs when one person intentionally establishes and maintains control over another, often escalating to intimate partner violence. This type of control can manifest in verbal, emotional, physical, psychological, and sexual abuse, leaving the victim feeling frightened, isolated, and reliant on the abuser. Have you ever heard of Stockholm syndrome? It is described as a condition where hostages develop a psychological bond with their captors, resulting from power imbalances in abusive relationships, hostage-taking, and kidnapping.

If you are experiencing any of these signs, it is best to seek professional help from a therapist specializing in gaslighting or coercive control.

Entryway Exchanges

In most mediation cases I work on, couples tend to avoid crucial conversations. They are undoubtedly tough to have. Either they have fought so much that now they are choosing not to engage for fear of confrontation, or perhaps they are avoiding conversations altogether.

These critical conversations can range from simple topics, such as how much money to spend on their children, to more complex issues, such as disrespect in the relationship and lack of financial contribution to the family.

Instead of deep conversations, they are left with only entryway exchanges. They continue to pass by each other in the hallway, like ships passing in the night. And perhaps the hallway is the only place they touch. In their bed, they might as well each be on the other side of an ocean. They may talk about the weather, who is picking up the kids, or what is for dinner if they talk at all. Unfortunately, failure to continue deep and meaningful conversations can lead to resentment by one or both parties.

It can be frustrating if you feel like you're the only one putting effort into your marriage, and your partner is unwilling to meet you halfway. They might refuse to consider couples therapy or dismiss your suggestions, such as having a date night. This situation might feel like a waste of your time and energy. And the truth is, you can't force anyone to change but yourself. The only thing you can do is change how you react. When trying so hard and putting in the extra effort, be careful not to lose yourself.

Doorway of Deception

According to my survey, 38% of the respondents mentioned that their marriage ended due to infidelity. Even the suspicion of infidelity can have a destructive impact on even the strongest of marriages. It's important to acknowledge that each individual and each marriage will respond differently to such a situation.

A significant number of my clients have faced infidelity in their marriages. For some individuals, adultery is a dealbreaker that can swiftly terminate their marriage. For others, it may linger between them for years. Yet some can reconstruct and form a new, healthy relationship.

One of my interviewees shared, "I wished my eyes were open wider." She felt like she had blinders on that prevented her from acknowledging and addressing the ongoing infidelity. After filing for divorce three times (with two failed attempts where she backed out), she finally felt ready and financially secure enough to proceed. She expressed how she wished she had followed through sooner, as it took her almost ten years to get out, but the third time was the charm. Only then did she find the strength she needed to move forward. I'm glad she did, as it eventually led her to an open door with a room filled with happiness.

Deciding how to move forward after an affair is a personal choice. No right or wrong answer exists, and each person's experience varies. Take your time and follow your heart.

Threshold of Discord

Early on in a relationship, passion can hide differences that can lead to potential incompatibility in the long run. It is not uncommon for couples to have differing political views, desires about having children, or other important matters.

Marital schism, also known as marital discord or marital disharmony[4] , is a state of tension in a marriage caused by a divergence of the spouses' mentalities, interests, and values. Marital schism is characterized by a lack of communication, cooperation, and consensus between the partners, leading to feelings of insecurity, unhappiness, and frustration in the marriage. The psychological consequences of marital schism can be severe,

---

4. https://encyclopedia.arabpsychology.com/marital-schism/

leading to decreased mental well-being, marital distress, and even divorce (Garrido, Gomil & Álvarez, 2019).

When someone notices disharmony in their marriage, they may start seeing it everywhere, leading to problems. Noticeable differences can escalate into explosive conflicts, resembling a collision of a volcano and a tornado within the Grand Canyon. Disharmony can cause issues when one spouse expects the other's viewpoint to change magically; when it doesn't, it can create a significant divide. What was once a blurred boundary, is now a shift from harmony to discord.

Gateway of Support

According to a recent study by *Forbes Advisor* lack of support was cited as the primary cause of divorce, with 43% of respondents attributing it to their decision.[5]

Previously, it was common for one spouse to work outside the home while the other managed household responsibilities. However, in many modern households, both spouses now have to work due to the current economic conditions. Additionally, there is an increase in the number of tasks to be done, especially with children being involved in multiple activities that require the parents to be responsible for transporting them and picking them up. This results in both parents feeling exhausted by the end of the day, eagerly awaiting the weekend, which unfortunately often ends up being filled with errands, chores, and more activities. It can seem like there is no time for each other.

You may long for family support. Some are lucky to have active grand-parents who want to be part of their lives or supportive friends and family. If you don't have a lot of support, dealing with all that comes from finances to family falls on only the two of you. It can either strengthen or stress the two of you. How you are able to work together can be the deciding factor.

---

5. https://www.forbes.com/advisor/legal/divorce/common-causes-divorce/

Unlocking Different Parenting Portals

Arguably, the most critical aspect of many marriages is raising healthy and happy children. This job has many challenges. Don't you wish there was a manual for parenting?

Each parent has a unique approach or method to parenting, just like every key opens a different door. Differences may not lead to divorce, as some parents find harmony in their differences and make it work in the children's best interest. However, problems can arise when both parents have different methods, leading to conflict and stress that may strain the relationship.

The Door is Slowly Swinging Shut

At the beginning of a relationship, you hang on to each other's every word and can't wait to spend more time with them. We all desire to engage with each other's lives and interests. Imagine your partner's dismay when you stop caring about what they do or no longer want to spend time with them. Some distractions might be understandable, especially when children enter the picture.

The term "silent killer" describes a subtle but destructive issue that can gradually undermine a marriage's foundation without drawing attention to itself. I understand that it can be overlooked for years, yet it can ultimately lead to the breakdown of a relationship. In simpler terms, it may seem easier to do nothing.

You wish they would say something.

They wish you would say something.

But no one says anything.

After a period of inactivity, when your needs are no longer being met, and there is no excitement or connection, you might find that even phone calls at night no longer grab your attention, and you can't make them jealous no matter how hard you tried. It's tough when you feel there's no hope for the relationship. Building a future together can be incredibly challenging, especially if you and your partner have different goals and plans. It's even more complicated when your partner seems self-centered and lacks empathy, and your emotions are disregarded. It can feel like life is tearing you apart and shattering your heart.

Have you heard about *The 5 Love Languages* by Gary Chapman? I did not hear about this until I was in therapy to help me deal with my divorce. I read the book and took the quiz at https://5lovelanguages.com/

The five languages of love are:

1. Quality Time

2. Receiving Gifts

3. Personal touch

4. Acts of Service

5. Words of Affirmation

This resonated with me. My language of love is Quality Time. They say you can get a lot of insight into someone with what they complain about not receiving. As you can imagine, if you and your partner do not speak each other's love language, your metaphorical bucket can feel empty, and your partner's can, too. Just like not having enough food in your belly, it can make you feel exhausted, leaving you with no will to fight.

Couples who rarely engage in conflict may have reached a point where they are stuck in unproductive patterns, causing them to stop trying to connect with their partner. This withdrawal may be due to a history of unfulfilled needs.

Reflection Points

- Have you tried couples therapy?

- If not, do you want to try couples therapy?

- If yes, is your spouse willing to try couples therapy?

- How do you feel couples therapy will help your marriage?

- What are the reasons behind your unhappiness?

- Are you willing to put in the effort to make things work?

- Do you have an intimate connection with your spouse? If not, why do you think that is?

- Do you have hope for your relationship?

- If you're contemplating staying in your marriage, consider why you want to stay.

- What would be a dealbreaker that would cause you to leave?

- If you had to, are you willing to forgive and let go of the past?

- What is the advice your family and close friends give you? Reflect on what their insights mean to you.

- Does staying in the marriage align with your values?

- Are you compromising your integrity or well-being by staying? Ensure your decision feels authentic to who you are.

- What is your love language?

- Does your partner speak your language?

- What do you think your partner's love language is?

- Can you speak their language?

"You have power over your mind,

not outside events.

Realize this, and you will find strength."

— **Marcus Aurelius**

2

Finding Strength

DISCOVERING A STRONG DOOR

Y ou must have various forms of strength when going through a trying time. Anyone who has said, "Divorce is the easy way out," has likely never been through a divorce. I was with someone the other day at a networking event, and she asked, "Do people just give up too easily nowadays? Is that why the divorce rate is so high?" My answer was a resounding "no!"

Divorce can be an incredibly tough experience, and it's understandable why anyone going through it might find it so challenging. It's a difficult journey, especially for those who have made the difficult decision to pursue a divorce. During this time, it's important to nurture your resilience, show kindness to yourself and others, and find the courage to face the tough decisions and obstacles ahead. It takes great strength to pick yourself up after being knocked down; determination is key during this challenging time.

Close your eyes and imagine the "strongest" person you know. Do you see someone who accomplishes the most daring feats, or do you envision someone who handles setbacks easily, confidently, and toughly?

I watched a video by National Geographic[1] that depicted extraordinary courage. Explorer Bertie Gregory has spent the last decade traveling

---

1. https://www.youtube.com/watch?v=ru-JG89w8us

in far-off regions, this time to the Antarctic Peninsula. He caught footage of a flock of baby penguins taking their first swim (called fledging). These penguins were jumping off sea ice into the cold water below. These ice cliffs were upwards of 50 feet high. One by one, they leaped! Free-falling into big chunks of ice in the water. To me, it sounds like they were falling into chunks of concrete. Imagine? And guess what? They did not just survive but popped up going, "I can swim." That right there is courage.

Granted, those penguins probably didn't put as much thought into diving into the water as we do when we dive into divorce, but they are still courageous.

I named my business "Finding Strength with Shell" to provide my clients with motivation and strength to overcome the most challenging times. I aim to offer support in the face of obstacles and help them overcome challenges while ensuring they are kind to themselves.

That is why I became a Certified Divorce Financial Analyst®, mediator, and Certified Divorce Coach®. I help people navigate the divorce process so that they can make good decisions and move into the next chapter easily and gracefully. I am not a lawyer, so any perspective I provide is on my existing knowledge of finances and divorce and not from a legal viewpoint. Divorce decisions are so profoundly personal. Seeking professional advice tailored to your specific circumstances is paramount.

My superpower is my financial expertise and ability to meet my clients where they are in their journey and help them move forward. I have deep work experience with over 20 years in the financial services industry, a master's in accounting, specific technical knowledge of finances through a divorce, and strong communication skills. I use a positive approach when working with my clients.

Strength comes from doing what you thought you could not do. Here are some ways to find strength in these trying times.

1. **<u>Use your fears to strengthen you</u>** – Tackle them head-on, just like the baby penguin leaping into the waters. Now, I don't want you to jump into cold waters because you are not a penguin but identify your fears and take baby steps to walk through them. What do I mean by identifying your fears? Call them out! Say out loud what you are fearing. Now that you know your worries, don't let them rule you.

2. **<u>See yourself as brave</u>** – If you envision yourself as fearless, you are more likely to act courageously.

3. **<u>Keep moving forward</u>** – Don't allow your fears to set you back. There will be days when anxiety takes over, but don't let it defeat you. Get back on your feet the next day and continue towards your bright future.

4. **<u>Look for support</u>** – Surround yourself with friends, family, and professionals who lift you up, remind you of your strengths, and motivate you to keep moving in the right direction. Remember, it's not about the quantity of people in your life but the quality of those relationships that matter. Avoid spending time with those who enjoy gossiping and talking negatively about others. What they do to others is likely what they will do to you. Instead, seek individuals who inspire and support you to become your best self. It's better to be alone than be in toxic people's company.

Hesitating in the Hallway

Are you hesitant to initiate a divorce, or do you make excuses to avoid it altogether, even though you want to end your marriage? Perhaps you are uncertain, waiting for the perfect moment to act. Maybe you are worried about hurting your spouse and hoping your feelings will dissipate on their own. Or maybe they are charismatic and keep telling you they will change, and you want it so bad that you hold on. Alternatively, you might need help to gather the courage to bring up the topic of divorce. The truth is, there is never a "right time" to initiate a divorce. Delaying this decision, however, may come at a cost.

Financially, it's important to note that remaining married to your spouse can expose you to debts, even after separation. Until the divorce is final, creditors can hold both spouses accountable. Moreover, acquiring new property during separation can further complicate the situation.

While you may trust your spouse, you must understand that bad decisions happen during times like this; people are at their worst. It is not necessarily them, or I don't like to think that. I want to believe it is their grief. I have seen people running up debt or failing to make payments, which can significantly impact their spouse's future. You do not want this to affect your ability to purchase property or obtain housing due to a poor credit history.

Take my client, Mandy, as an example. We worked together to organize her finances and assess possible settlement options during her divorce. While we were in the process, her spouse expressed his intention to buy a new home for himself. The purchase of a new home raised a significant financial concern for Mandy. I advised her that using marital funds for a down payment could tie up their joint finances in a property she couldn't access. Although the new home might be considered marital property, her main goal was to secure enough funds to support herself in the future. I recommended that she discuss this matter with her husband during an upcoming conversation and ensure that he kept the new home purchase off the table until the divorce was finalized.

It's worth mentioning that delaying a divorce can impact spousal or child support and other divorce terms. Therefore, it's crucial to consider these factors and make informed decisions for you and your financial well-being. If you have never put yourself first before, do it now. I know you will have no regrets.

Reflection Points

- How can you gain strength to move forward?

- How can you use your fears to strengthen you?

- Does your support system lift you up?

"Divorce isn't such a tragedy.

A tragedy's staying in an unhappy marriage

and teaching your children

the wrong things about love."

- Jennifer Weiner

3

Facing Your Fears

WHICH DOOR SHOULD YOU CHOOSE?

There comes a point in every struggle where you must decide. Imagine life as a series of interconnected rooms, each with its own door. Sometimes, we enter a room unexpectedly, and it changes our course. Which door will you choose?

My favorite poet, Robert Frost, talked about this contemplation in his poem "The Road Not Taken."

> *"And be one traveler, long I stood*
> *I looked down one as far as I could*
> *To where it bent in the undergrowth"*

Was he contemplating divorce? He may have been, at least; it sounds like that. He stood long, looked down as far as he could, and decided to go down one of the two roads. It can take time to determine the best road to travel down.

As you consider your decision, please remember to be kind to yourself. Since starting my business, I've noticed many are hard on themselves. I get that, as I was, too. A question often asked is, "This sounds terrible, doesn't it?" But the truth is, no way. You are only human, and it's okay to have feelings. Remember that certain circumstances led you to this place.

You don't have to justify your actions to anyone—not your friends, family, or spouse.

It's natural to expect some adverse reactions to the news. Be prepared. Take a moment to reflect on your journal and recall the events that led you here. If they were in your shoes, they would react similarly. You're not alone in feeling this way.

The more you focus on your fear, the less control you have over your situation. Do not let fear keep you from focusing solely on yourself and how to change your behavior and perceptions rather than worry about your spouse.

It's essential to recognize that no one wakes up one day and decides they want a divorce. It's a gradual process. I hesitate to label these experiences as stages because they are not linear journeys. A breakdown in a relationship is a rollercoaster of emotions, often involving attempts to leave or reconcile before a final separation. I went through this in my marriage. It took about two years from the time he left me at the party to when we decided to pursue divorce officially. Studies show that the emotional readiness for divorce can take anywhere from one and a half to five years. It may sound surprising, but that's the reality.

Of my survey respondents, who were all women, 90% said that they initiated the divorce, and most, 36%, only took a few months before they talked to their spouse about desiring a divorce. A whopping 26% took over three years before they even mentioned it to their spouse, with a few waiting almost **ten years!** Most state that they stayed at least a year longer than they should have.

Why do so many stay so long? Fear! Fear of the unknown and the known. And knowing that others are getting divorced every day does not make it any less frightening.

It can be complicated for those outside of the relationship to understand why women stay, especially if they are in an abusive relationship. Abuse is not just physical; it can be mental, emotional, or even financial. The constant question is, "Why doesn't she just leave?" The answer is much more complicated than it appears. It is easy for others to cast stones when they haven't been in this situation before.

My office has a sign that says, "Face your fears and do it anyway." I want you to remember that time is precious. Don't waste that time on someone who doesn't realize you are a treasure, too!

Staying in an unhealthy relationship can include many factors, some of which encourage conditions that keep you insecure, dependent, and socially isolated. You deserve to feel safe and happy, so it's vital to love yourself enough to create a brighter future for you and your children.

Here are some reasons why some may stay in their marriage longer than they would like. Most of these fears can be paralyzing, but let's explore ways to release some fear and develop an ability to cope. Perhaps there is something here you can relate to that will give you some hope for the future.

Locking in Financial Stability

It would be no surprise if the fear of your financials after divorce has your stomach in knots. Money can be a relationship's downfall or can be the reason couples stay together. CNBC reports that 23% of couples remain together mainly because of money constraints.[1] It would be nice if all couples were on the same page with their finances—setting goals and understanding their budgets and investments together. Unfortunately, that is not reality. In some marriages, one of the partners handles the family's finances, leaving the other in the dark, either by choice or happenstance. Take my client, Lisa; she allowed her husband to handle all the finances. They have been married for 20 years, and a lot has changed. Most statements and invoices are now digitized, making it more challenging to locate them.

Roles are traditionally established when couples first marry or even start living together. One spouse may take out the garbage regularly, and

---

1.
https://www.cnbc.com/2023/03/31/financial-dependency-23percent-of-couples-stay-bec ause-of-money.html#:~:text=Money%20can%20be%20a%20relationship%E2%80%99s%2 0downfall%3B%20it%20can,dependency%2C%20according%20to%20a%20new%20repor t%20by%20LendingTree .

another does the laundry. This is true of financial responsibilities, too. Every so often, my clients, even mediation clients, are unaware of their financial portfolios and have never looked at their credit reports. If this sounds like you, you are not alone! Heck, I know Financial Professionals who could be better with their finances. It is said, "The cobbler has no shoes."

I had a phone call this morning with a potential mediation client, Malcolm. I had previously had a conversation with his wife, Allison. When Malcolm first said hello, his voice was soft. I thought, "Well, he is on the doorstep of divorce, right? Most have sadness in their voice during such a time, especially if they do not want it." Throughout our phone call, we ventured into many different topics. One that stands out to me is our conversation about his relationship with money. Everyone has a relationship with money. Good or bad, happy or sad. He told me that although he was a financial professional, he wasn't good with his finances. He was embarrassed to say it but eventually felt comfortable mentioning it. He didn't budget, hated opening the mail, and didn't pay his water bill on time.

Wait, what? Did he just say that he hated opening his mail? Yup! That's a thing. I know this one a little too well. I hate my mail. Yes, I get anxious opening my mail, too. I know where this stems from. When I was younger and living with my then-partner, my first husband, sometimes he would get the mail. I didn't have an aversion to it back then. I probably didn't think much of it. I trusted him. I came to find out he was hiding mail from me—one piece of mail, in particular, "the dreaded credit card statement." You see, everything was paper back then. You got all your bills and invoices in the mail; nothing was electronic. I know, it's hard to imagine. We even paid for it all by check. What a concept.

He was running up the credit card without telling me. To make matters worse, this was MY credit card, and he was just an authorized user. That was a big mistake on my part. He was intercepting the mail and not paying the bill, not even the minimum payment amount. He was avoiding it. He had bought a house with his brother, and they were trying to flip it (this was back before the concept of flipping houses was common). He hoped to get a payday from the flipped home and pay it off before I realized what had happened, but he wasn't getting that payday; he was accumulating more and more and more. And then, one day, I was the one who got the mail. What a shock—and what a financial disaster! By the time divorce was on our doorstep (this was not the only reason; there were many). The debt still lingered, and I wound up with half. My state, Connecticut, is considered a fair and equitable state.

What does that mean? They air on the side of fairness, which does not mean equal, but most usually start with 50/50 for marital property. Looking back, I know my agreement wasn't fair, but I wanted out. It was not a good move on my part, as had I advocated for myself and got what I deserved, I would have been much better off. Now, I try to help clients avoid the mistakes I made. I deserved better. Ahh, to go back and renegotiate that agreement now. I want a do-over. I wouldn't have left myself so financially strapped. That winter, I was living paycheck to paycheck and couldn't afford to furnish my apartment or even afford Christmas presents for my family; it was horrible.

You have one chance to make your agreement right, and the time is now. Unfortunately, there are no givebacks or do-overs.

Here is the thing about finances and marriage. Most of us learned about finances when we grew up. We didn't learn any skills in school, and if you didn't have a good financial role model, how would you obtain these skills? Most of what we do with our finances is learned behavior and skills learned through our years on this earth. These experiences create our unique connection with money, which is emotional, just like any other relationship we have.

Then, there comes a time when you meet your spouse and come together. Your spouse potentially has different viewpoints and feelings about money. Together, you develop a financial family. The two of you may see your finances differently. Differently doesn't mean wrong, but it may lead to conflict and struggles if you are at odds.

Money is a source of pride or comfort for some or, at the other end of the spectrum, shame, guilt, or even stress. Money has been our society's connection since the dawn of time. We all strive for financial freedom, and many aim to build wealth.

Money differences emerge when two people consider how they should disseminate the money from their budget (if there is one), how to save for retirement, and how much debt to take on.

Imagine one spouse having a stressful or conservative relationship with money, so they want to save, and the other spouse feeling that money is in an unlimited supply, so they want to spend it all, and they do. The spender might have a sense of pride and want to show off to their friends with nice cars or clothes, but the other doesn't feel comfortable with that approach. This could create stress for the couple, especially if it keeps happening and the couple starts to accumulate debt. These differences may cause anxiety, to say the least.

Other stressors for the relationship can be job loss, if one spouse is viewed as an inadequate money maker, or there are control-related issues. Mistrust and resentment can then become commonplace between spouses.

We shouldn't confuse this with financial abuse. Financial abuse displays itself in various deceptive ways, deeply rooted in manipulation, power, and control. When a spouse is financially abusing their partner, they are usually limiting their access or utilization of funds, frequently prioritizing their own needs. Victims feel trapped and dependent on their abuser. Financial abuse can display itself as financial infidelity, where one spouse is deceitful in the handling of funds, which can include undisclosed debts, hidden assets, and bad decisions (i.e., gambling). Financial abuse can be a devasting form of intimate partner violence. Once discovered, the victim should seek support to remove themselves from harm's way. Safety should be the number one priority, and a local domestic violence shelter can help you create a plan to leave an unhealthy, abusive relationship.

National Domestic Violence Hotline
1 (800) 799–7233
Available 24 hours a day, seven days a week
via phone and online chat

As you prepare yourself and your finances to escape abuse, be cautious and proceed carefully and at the right time. Create a go bag with an emergency stash of important documents, financial records, clothing, and cash. Find a safe place to store it somewhere your partner can't access it, such as with a trusted friend who knows your situation or in a bank safety deposit box.

It is always a good idea to have a separate emergency fund, whether you are in an abusive relationship or not. You may already have an account, or you can create one. If you can't do this safely, ask a trusted friend or family member to help you keep your emergency fund safe.

It's recommended that you create a fund to cover the expenses you may incur while leaving a relationship and re-establishing yourself. You can contribute to this fund using your income or work bonuses or by seeking financial assistance from friends, family, or support organizations. It's essential to set aside enough money to cover your projected costs.

Steps to safeguard your finances once you leave:

1. **Pull your credit report**. If you are concerned that your partner may accumulate additional debt under your name, you can freeze your credit to protect against fraud.

2. **Change your passwords**. If you previously shared bank or credit card account login info, update those passwords.

3. **Contact your banks and credit cards.** Alert them of the situation.

4. **Change your health insurance coverage** if necessary. If you have health insurance through your abusive partner's employment, for example, investigate alternative coverage through your employer or visit Healthcare.gov to find your state-specific Health Insurance Marketplace or Medicaid.

5. **<u>Monitor and safeguard your credit rating and social security number</u>**. Choose a respectable institution like LifeLock by Norton.

Reflection Points

- What are your main concerns about your finances?

- What are your financial triggers?

- What are your financial goals for the future?

Leaning on the Door for Support

In some circumstances, including if you are a stay-at-home parent or make significantly less than your spouse, you may feel particularly financially dependent on your spouse.

You may be concerned about the income that was once used to maintain one home, and a specific lifestyle may now be needed to support two separate households.

If you feel tempted to cling to this way of life, that is understandable; working with a Certified Divorce Financial Analyst® (CDFA®) before walking down the path of divorce can help you prepare for the future. A CDFA® can help you know what to expect. They can give you information and ensure you know all the short- and long-term implications of specific decisions. This preparation will help you save money in the divorce process by reducing billable hours and making meetings more efficient. The most significant benefit is to release your financial fears and reassure you that everything will be okay. You will have the right professional by your side to help you make good decisions. This also ensures you are not alone.

Reflection Points

- What is financially occurring in your marriage that makes you fear divorce?

- Knowing that the next chapter may have some financial constraints, what is something you could start doing now to prepare yourself?

- What are some financial statements that you need to gain access to?

Always Keep the Door Open

It is natural to worry about our children and how they are going to handle their parents' divorce. And many parents believe that divorce will harm their children. On the contrary and statistically speaking, staying together for the children is never a good idea. If you think that staying in an unhappy marriage for the sake of your kids is the right thing to do, think again. Your children's perception of relationships and marriages will be heavily influenced by what they see in your relationship. If your relationship is unhealthy and unhappy, it may leave a lasting negative impact on your children. Therefore, it's essential to consider the long-term consequences of staying in an unhappy marriage.

Divorce doesn't hurt children; conflict does. The best present you can give them is to encourage open communication and an environment of love and support.

The thought of not seeing your child every day can make you immobilized, but moving forward can sometimes be the best thing you can do for yourself and your family. If the children have been mainly your responsibility, divorce presents the ability for parents to share parenting and finally work together. Of course, this is always in the best interest of the children. There is no longer one primary parent but two with clear expectations and guidelines. Synchronicity!

Something that comes up often is that one parent worries about the other parent's ability to care for their children. They are scared that the other parent will not adequately parent the children.

Take my clients, Steve and Melonie. Steve was never an active parent. He admitted that he never helped with homework, ensured the children were fed adequately, or drove them to activities. He let Melonie handle it all. Melonie was concerned they would not be cared for properly when the children were with Steve. He understood her concern, so the pair opted for a modified parenting schedule until Steve could prove that he would actively do what was suitable for the children. Once Melonie could ensure the children were safe and cared for, the schedule would expand for Steve. We documented both options in their divorce agreement.

And, yes, how you do your divorce matters. Children need stability and consistency from nurturing and loving parents. Opt to utilize mediation or collaborative divorce to complete the process. These alternative dispute resolution methods significantly benefit children, as you will make decisions for your family's future, ultimately leading to better co-parenting. Even though the family might look slightly different, the parents in this picture will be effective co-parents with reduced stress and conflict.

Reflection Points

- Are you currently demonstrating to your children a healthy relationship/marriage?

- What would you think if your child were in a relationship or marriage like yours?

- What are you teaching them by staying in this relationship?

- What would make you feel more confident about sharing parenting with your spouse?

A Doorway to Connection

Are you concerned your friends and community will treat you like you have cooties? Or maybe your spouse is so charismatic that people will believe them over you because they don't know what they are really like? Even though society has come a long way, there are still those who cast judgment on divorcing individuals and couples. Some may feel divorce is contagious or a threatening storm that will eventually pass through their neighborhood and come into their home unannounced. Who's to blame them, seeing as the divorce rate is so high (40-50%) and even higher if this is your second (60%) or third marriage (73%)? [2] That threat is real.

Remember: Divorce and moving on are okay, but staying where you are not valued and appreciated is not OK. Sometimes, it is better to move on than hold on to someone who doesn't get you and realize what a gem you are.

You know why you are considering divorce. Robert Frost might advise you to let go and give yourself the greatest gift: unconditional acceptance and love. Are you pretending to be "living"? Treating yourself first is essential for you to be there for others. The sentiment reminds me of flying on an airplane. They inform you at the beginning of the flight that if something goes wrong, you must wear an oxygen mask before caring for others. I encourage you to wear your oxygen mask before pursuing anything further.

Unfortunately, worrying about something you can't change will take away time you will never get back. I wasted many years overthinking everything, so I want to give those years to you.

The truth is that the ones who cast judgment are not your people. And just like the evening news, you will only be a current news story

---

for a short while. Something new will come up, and that will be what they all discuss. What can be wonderful are the people you find when divorce is knocking on your door. You may have true friends you know will be supportive, especially those who have been here themselves and understand what you are going through.

These people will:

- Make you feel safe in their presence.

- Listen without judgment.

- Support your future.

- They want you to be happy, even if they have to travel on a bumpy road with you (not just bumps, but potholes, too!)

You will find your people when you least expect it. At a random networking event, a divorce support group, when you pick up a long-lost hobby, or from an acquaintance that you spend some time with and unexpectedly become close friends.

One of my survey respondents discussed how much she anticipated her professional career to be tough after the divorce. She expected the doors to be shut in her face, have no seat at the table, and she was sure that the corporate ladder would break in two! Corporate America can be a challenging environment in and of itself, but after divorcing, you worry about the potential impact on your career and financial well-being. Perception can hold you back, but don't let it. My professional life was my point of refuge during my divorce. The consistency of going to the office, working hard, and accomplishing goals gave me purpose during trying times.

My survey respondent knew she needed to improve her financial situation after her divorce. She was determined to make this happen. She decided to work on advancing her career at her company. And that is precisely what she did. She didn't have this opportunity before in her marriage because she was the primary caregiver, so getting out of work on time was crucial. Now, she was sharing custody of her children with their father and had a few days a week to devote to her career. That meant potentially staying late, taking on more tasks, and putting in the extra effort. In a matter of thirteen years, in a male-dominated occupation, she broke the glass ceiling and entered the C-suite.

Instead of stifling you, divorce can open doors to new opportunities.

Reflection Points

- What are your most immediate concerns around the social and professional stigma of divorce?

- Do you feel stifled in your career because of your role in your marriage?

Turning the Key to a Fresh Start

We all wish we had a crystal ball to see our life post-divorce, as it would make it much easier to put that foot forward. Am I right? We are still waiting for someone to invent a tool to see into the future. Elon, get on that, will you?

Your lives are so intertwined that you can't imagine life without the other being a significant part. The shared responsibilities like pets, children, and mortgages might make life without them seem daunting.

Life is not over after divorce; it transforms and can provide fantastic opportunities. Please remember that your current anxiety may dissipate, and focusing on the new possibilities may help. This new chapter may bring unique opportunities to reconnect with personal interests or hobbies that may have been put on the back burner during your marriage, or you may have the chance to find something you love to do that will make you truly happy. You know the saying, "Don't do it because you have to; do it because you want to"? Now is the time to embrace this and do something that makes you feel good. Maybe it is simply that you will have more time with your friends, go to the gym more often, or go back to school to earn a degree! It may be hard to see now, but your future has endless possibilities.

When I divorced, I had no idea what to do with my free time. At first, this was hard. I spent too much time lying around and crying. Eventually, I came up with some ideas to fill my time. I went to the gym, got a manicure or pedicure, and started my Certified Divorce Coach training. It was a transformational experience, and it has positively impacted my life in incredible ways, not to mention taking up some free time.

I recently read an article about a newly divorced woman who went on the Nextdoor App and posted that she was looking for other freshly divorced women to meet for coffee. They all met and connected to form valuable friendships. What a great idea!

Have you heard that most women experience a "Glow-up" after their divorce? It's a thing! They transform and become healthier and happier. I believe this is because they finally have time for self-care and reflection. If nothing else, remember this and keep it in your sights. You will get there.

You can also find a Divorce Recovery Coach in your area. Working with a Divorce Recovery Coach is a great way to move beyond your grief, explore your new identity, and create a life you love. Get some help from someone who gets you! If they have a group program, it would be an excellent opportunity to connect with other women experiencing the same thing.

Check out www.unlimitedyoullc.com for some great resources.

Reflection Points

- Does your spouse bring you happiness?

- When you daydream about your future, is your spouse a part of the picture?

- What is something you can't wait to do once your divorce is final?

- What is something you can see yourself doing once you are divorced?

- How can you envision spending time for personal growth and enrichment?

- What would be a way for you to rediscover your identity?

Do Not Barricade the Exit

Feelings of shame are not uncommon in an emotionally challenging experience. Individuals may grapple with self-blame and a sense of failure after divorce. Shame often arises when people feel they are falling short of expectations or ideals, whether their own, their family's, or society's. In the context of divorce, it can stem from the belief that they have somehow failed to maintain their marriage.

The traditional wedding vow of "'til death do us part" and religious ideals can create immense tension and anxiety. However, we all know and recognize that relationships are complex, and maintaining a successful marriage over a lifetime is difficult. People can change over time. While contemplating, you may often recall how the relationship was at the beginning and the love you shared.

Again, as Robert Frost writes, "Nature's first green is gold." Like in a relationship, it is gold when you start dating and falling in love, but it is hard to hold that hue. Nothing gold can stay. Either or both of your needs may have evolved. That's nature, and that's natural.

Many couples put in significant effort to make their marriage work. Sometimes, despite their best efforts, they realize that their emotional stress outweighs the comfort and security the relationship provides.

Let's face it: no one wants to "fail" at anything. This is not a failure. This is a chance to learn, grow, and become the best version of yourself. You may find you are lamenting with a glimmer of hope. It is similar to a butterfly's beauty. A marriage's end might not be a complete loss, but rather the ability to find solace in the memory of what once was.

Contemplating divorce and the divorce process itself is so personal. It is hard sometimes to see the forest through the trees. Talking to a mental health professional can help you process some of your emotions, release the shame, and help you move forward.

Reflection Points

- Are your needs different than when you first met your spouse?

- What are the pros of staying in your marriage?

- What are the cons of staying in your marriage?

- What would help you acknowledge that this doesn't equate to failure?

- What did you learn from your relationship?

- Did you experience any growth during your relationship?

- What are you grateful for that came from your marriage?

The Door to Knowledge is Open

It's true! No one knows much about divorce until it is at your doorstep. Divorce is not a game but an arena where the rules are not readily known, except by a chosen few (divorce professionals). I understand that dealing with the lack of information or knowledge about divorce can be a significant concern. Now is the time to take a moment to gather as much information as possible before diving into the divorce process. Remember, being prepared puts your best foot forward.

One of my survey respondents said she wished she had pursued educating herself about divorce and her rights. She felt so stressed about what she didn't know and accepted what she was given and felt like it was "good enough." Now, looking back, she feels swindled.

Each state is unique and has specific requirements and laws—for instance, residency requirements for filing for divorce. Before filing, you may need to have lived in the state for a certain period (e.g., six months, nine months, a year). Familiarize yourself with state laws governing property division, child custody, and child support.

You can do this by attending events given by divorce professionals and having complimentary consultations with divorce professionals in your area. Facebook Events and Eventbrite are great places to start. Having a consultation does not mean you will begin the divorce process any time soon; it just means you are getting all your ducks in a row.

Reflection Points

- How can you research the laws and requirements for divorce in your state?

- What events come up on Eventbrite that are divorce-related?

- What are the events on Facebook that you can attend?

The Family Door is Always Ajar

Thinking of your family not being together to share memories and space can be unfathomable. However, you can still maintain a sense of family unity, especially for the children's sake.

Divorce can be emotionally charged. Be patient with yourself, your ex-spouse, and the process. Healing takes time, and patience helps maintain a stable environment for the family.

Regardless of the circumstances, strive for civility. One of my survey respondents shared how that made her life and her kids' lives easier. An attorney gave her some advice: "Make the co-parenting work no matter what." That meant that she should try her best to make it successful at all costs and strive to be amicable. Co-parenting children across separate locations or homes requires mutual respect and a commitment to positive communication. Remember, it's about keeping the children's best interests in mind. Their well-being should help guide custody, visitation, and communication decisions.

Furthermore, try to keep them away from adult conversations as much as possible and not to put them in the middle of the two of you. If you have a question for the other parent, ask the other parent (not the children) if you can and try your best to obtain this behavior from the other parent.

During my co-parenting adventure, a few instances arose when my daughter didn't want to go to her father's house at the agreed-upon time. Initially, I supported her decision to stay with me and make her own decisions. Looking back, I did this because being apart from her was hard. However, I eventually realized that my preference for her to stay with me was not in her best interest. As a result, I started encouraging her to go to her father's house. I'm glad I did, as it has brought them closer together. Now that she is older, they want to spend time together without any persuasion on my part. That is all I could ask for.

There's no one-size-fits-all solution, so be flexible and tread forward with an open mind.

Remember, even after divorce, a family can find ways to stay connected and supportive of one another.

Are you having difficulty trying to find the right words to tell your children you are getting divorced? Remember the acronym "KISS" (Keep it simple and straightforward).

1. **Be united** - Tell them together if you can! Show a united front with age-appropriate conversations.

2. **Be honest** – Tell them the truth about what is happening, without sharing all the gory details or placing any blame.

3. **Be reassuring** – Tell them you will both always love them, and this is not their fault.

4. **Be open** – See if they have any questions and ensure they can

talk to you whenever they want. You want them to be open to expressing their feelings and concerns.

Reflection Points

- What are good ways for your family to stay connected after your divorce?

Don't Let Their Haunted Tales Lock You Out of Your Dreams

It's interesting how people share their divorce stories with others who have gone through or are going through a similar situation. When I started working in the divorce field, it seemed like everyone had a story to tell. It's like when I was pregnant, and everyone shared the scary aspects of pregnancy, birth, or the terrible twos. It can be overwhelming, and you may feel like hiding under the covers until it's over. However, it's important to remember that everyone's situation is unique, and what happened to someone else may not happen to you. Unfortunately, people tend to focus on the negative aspects of life. It's rare to hear about the positive side of things. For instance, my ex-husband and I co-parent well, but I feel I am boasting if I mention it. I would love it if we could embrace those positives and give others uplifting and positive aspects, especially if it is not something they are pursuing but instead finding themselves on this threshold.

I used to work for a company with a slogan that said, "You can't predict; you can only prepare." I loved this slogan because I felt it was true for most things in life, particularly marriage and divorce. Sounds odd, but what if we maneuvered marriage like it just may happen? With the statistics the way they are, with almost 50 out of every 100 couples getting divorced, this doesn't sound too far-fetched. My daughters' pediatrician used to say, "If you're prepared, it's unlikely to happen."

Now, this wouldn't be foolproof, as some things being prepared may not solve, such as infidelity, abuse, and manipulation, as the best preparation doesn't help when trust is broken. But, maybe, just maybe, as we walk together through a marriage, we can take the proper steps so that if divorce ends on our doorstep, we will all be in a better position. Perhaps doing so might be preventative measures, after all.

What would this look like? Partners are on the same page with finances, understanding each other's relationship with money, having equal say in retirement contributions, having equal responsibilities at home, speaking nicely about each other in private and public, knowing each other's love language and speaking it, and communicating with one another about goals and expectations. I could probably go on and on.

There are courses when you get divorced, like parenting classes, which are required in some states. What if there was a required course when you are getting married that speaks about finances and communication strategies?

If we were keeping score—which we are not—as there are no winners in divorce, this would be another point for being prepared.

Reflection Points

- What are the top three things you fear will happen after divorce?

- What are the fears holding you back from making a decision?

- What are the consequences of remaining fearful?

"It is in the moments of your decision

that your destiny is shaped."

– Tony Robbins

4

Making a Decision

BEHIND EVERY DOOR LIES A PURPOSE

You've been thinking about it repeatedly, and your head is spinning with its possible ripple effects on your life. I know the indecision is weighing on you! Getting a divorce is—without question—one of the most significant and most complex decisions you'll ever make.

You can make this decision consciously or unconsciously. Of course, the conscious path is the best choice.

The unconscious path involves accepting life as it is, feeling like a hostage, and being unsure how to change it. You may hope your spouse becomes unhappy enough in your marriage to end it. This path almost always leads to a breaking point, resulting in impulsive decisions that can instantly implode. This path does not set you up for success, as it will not allow you enough time to prepare and be ready for what lies ahead.

To achieve a better outcome, taking a step back and evaluating things objectively is advisable. The more clarity you have in your decision-making, the fewer unexpected challenges you'll encounter on your journey ahead. Think of it like riding a roller coaster—the smoother the ride, the more enjoyable the experience will be! If you choose this method, you will most likely have more confidence and less confusion. You will, of course, decide in your own time and know when you know.

So, for now, while you are deciding, let's look at the phases of contemplation:

1. The consideration phase

2. The deliberating phase

3. The ruling phase

The earliest and most revocable phase is what I call the **consideration phase**. These thoughts can ebb and flow like the motion of the ocean. The idea of divorce may occasionally come into your mind, but it doesn't flood your thoughts. You may have moments of rationalization or clarity where you realize it is something you are starting to consider. Maybe your spouse doesn't speak to you kindly; you notice how controlling they are or how unhappy you feel. Whatever the reason, you think this is no longer the place you want to be. You know you deserve happiness but have concerns and maybe even wonder if staying is better. In this stage, you are in denial. You don't want to say it out loud, especially to your mother or best friend, as they may not understand, and if they knew, they might require you to act on it, as they will not be happy hearing the circumstances that brought you to this point. Sound familiar? This is probably the best time to engage a therapist. Talk therapy can do wonders for your soul. A therapist can help you understand the causes of your fear, and provide you with coping skills and strategies to support you on your journey.

The next phase is where S&%T becomes real. This is when someone gives more serious thought to divorce but is confused and conflicted. They are seriously **deliberating** in their mind and starting to talk with their most trusted supporters. Hopefully, they visit their therapist regularly, educate themselves, listen to podcasts, and pick up a good book or two (like this one!) This is the phase where most stay the longest, especially if you are a planner or overthinker. There is so much to consider that it could occupy your mind often. If you have ever heard of someone getting stuck, this is their space.

I had an excellent older client when I first started with divorce coaching. Her kids were grown, and she knew she and her husband were headed for divorce. They even mentioned the "D" word to each other, but he told her that if she wanted it, she needed to pull the trigger. Talk about pressure! But the thing was, she wasn't ready. I knew my goal was to help her get her head in the game. We discussed the pros and cons of staying and leaving, and it was clear to her after our conversations that the only thing holding her back was fear—fear of the unknown. Once she recognized her worries, we worked on how to overcome her fears so she could move forward.

If you haven't been here before, this phase can be a terrifying place with lots of ghosts and goblins, and sometimes, even the people you trust the most are trying to talk you out of leaving. That can be the scariest place of all.

If this is where you find yourself, know that fear is a normal and natural emotion that everyone experiences from time to time, especially when faced with the thought of divorce. Please try hard not to let it interfere with your everyday life. It's important to remember to take care of your emotional well-being during this difficult time. Your life may be anything but average at the moment. Having gone through some tough times and watching clients go through it daily, I believe life gives us these challenging moments to walk through so we can appreciate the good times. Life leads you on journeys we would never dream of going on if it were up to us. What you do during these challenging moments makes you into the person you are to become. Hopefully, falling in love with what you didn't even know you needed.

So, if you are struggling, there are some things you can do to cope and overcome. Here are some tips that might help you:

Talk, talk, and talk some more. Sharing your feelings with a friend, family member, or someone you trust can help you feel less alone and more supported.

Breathe. Now, I am not an expert in this, but it is helpful for me. Breathing deeply and slowly can help you relax and reduce the physical symptoms of fear and anxiety, such as racing heart, sweating, trembling, etc. You can try this simple exercise: inhale for four seconds, hold for two seconds, and exhale for six seconds. Repeat this for a few minutes until you feel calmer.

Exercise. Ha! We all know that physical activity can help you release tension, improve your mood, and boost your self-confidence ... *Blah!* Even though I know this, it is one of the hardest things for me when I am anxious, as I would much rather stuff my face with some potato chips. Try it (not the potato chips ... the exercise); it does clarify! I was a marathon runner with a group of running friends to keep me motivated. Exercise can be so freeing and can also help you find your people. Do whatever motivates you. Find a workout partner, take the dog out for a walk, or join the local gym where you can take a class that interests you.

Don't just stretch your body; include your mind, too. Read or listen to some uplifting books or podcasts. When I was going through my divorce, I had difficulty concentrating, and my brain felt foggy, but I was able to listen to some audible books when I was out for a walk with the dogs or on my way to work. Find someone you can resonate with and bring positivity into your life. I love Rachel Hollis and Mel Robbins and enjoy Michael J. Fox; he is always so positive even though he has traveled a tough road!

Reflection Points

- Who truly resonates with you?

- Who are the people who inspire you, motivate you, and make you feel alive?

Record. You notice I didn't write "journal." I did that intentionally, as I feel like when someone says it, I automatically don't want to do it. We contemplate when something unsettling happens, especially when we feel pain or suffering. If you're feeling hurt, angry, or outraged towards your spouse or the situation, it's a good time to start jotting down some notes and thoughts. Even if it's just documenting what's happening, write down your story and detail the events. This can help you gain clarity, sort things out, and serve as a reference point in the future to remind you why you made certain decisions. Writing can be a helpful tool in moving you forward and helps validate your choices.

I heard about the great idea of writing a letter to yourself! Whether it is to your past, present, or future self, you may have certain things you want to share with you. You can write a letter to your spouse (that you don't mail) to express any thoughts or wishes you may have for them that you never got a chance to express. Alternatively, you can write a letter to your children, reminding them they are always on your mind, or express your hopes and dreams for their future.

Reflection Points

- If you were to write a letter, who would you write it to?

- What would you say?

Speak Kindly to Yourself. Fear often comes from negative and unrealistic thoughts about yourself and your abilities. You might think you are incapable, not good enough, or not worthy of happiness. I have spent most of my lifetime doing this, and it has taken a lot of work to realize these thoughts are SO NOT TRUE! Don't let one negative thought define who you are; you have so many great qualities! Our thoughts have a significant impact on our happiness. Dwelling on negative, depressive thoughts can rob us of our joy. We must remind ourselves of our strengths, achievements, and positive qualities to challenge these thoughts. To cultivate positivity, we should maintain a positive mindset, which can enhance our overall mindset.

If you are experiencing negative self-talk, a coach can surely help; they will guide you in making good decisions and overcoming any challenges that may come your way.

Reflection Points

- What are your strengths?

- What are you grateful for?

- Is there a time in your past when you faced hardship? How did you overcome it?

Plan and Prepare

Sometimes, fear can motivate you to act! For example, people who are afraid of public speaking but are awarded a gig for speaking to a large audience—what do they do? They research their topic, ensure they know it like the back of their hand, and then rehearse until they feel comfortable. A clear and realistic plan can help you feel more confident and less fearful. Like me, a Personal Divorce Guide lets you prepare and organize! Being prepared makes you less afraid of what's to come and know what is needed to succeed! I will go into more detail on how to prepare in later chapters.

Self-care advice from a
PENGUIN

Find warmth among friends.
Appreciate snow days.
Go the extra mile.
Take long walks.
Stand together.
Keep your cool!

Remember, you are not alone, and you can overcome your fear and anxiety. You are brave and strong, and I believe in you.

The last phase is where your mind has been made up, usually after many internal struggles. The voices inside your head have been silenced. Thinking alone has never accomplished anything significant; eventually, you must act. This is the **ruling** phase, where a verdict will be reached!

Reflection Points

- There will always be many reasons to leave, but are there more reasons to stay?

- Do you feel your relationship is salvageable?

- Make a list of the current needs in your relationship. Does your partner fulfill the needs you identified?

- What was a previous issue that you navigated as a couple?

- How did you resolve this issue together?

"I sat with my anger long enough

until she told me her name was grief."

– C. S. Lewis

5

Processing Your Pain

CHANGE IS A DOOR THAT CAN ONLY OPEN FROM THE INSIDE

You've turned the knob of the door so often that it is now worn smooth by countless turns. Your mind spins with its possible ripple effects on your life. Getting a divorce is—without question—one of the most significant and most complex decisions you'll ever make. I am sure you have your reasons to be here! You've tried and tried, and now you feel frustrated, sad, triggered, resentful, or all the above. Whatever you do, do not allow that pain to build a home and call you broken. We aren't meant to live in this house; we are just here to visit. This is not the whole story; this is just a chapter. Allow the doorknob to act as your compass, guiding you to take that pain and shift it into Purpose. Purpose for you! Purpose for your children! Purpose for your family! As each door leads to a specific room, every experience we encounter serves a purpose—even if we don't immediately understand it.

This powerful statement reminds us to seek healing independently rather than relying on those who caused the pain.

How you deal with your pain is what sets you apart from others. Let's figure out how to channel your inner pain and embrace it. Take time to understand this anguish's impact on your emotions, thoughts, and, primarily, your actions. The pain will come, but don't let it consume you. Cry and vent it out, but don't let it take root in you. Seeing your discomfort can allow you to find your strength and courage. It may allow you to push through that pain from where you are now and get to where you need to be. Most progress is made when people do not feel like showing up, but they do it anyway.

That is perseverance! That is determination!

Penguins symbolize courage and fortitude, demonstrating that even in the darkest moments, we can persevere toward our destiny.

Don't let what happened make you vengeful. Vengefulness and rage do not let you operate with a clear mind.

I'll admit that I had a hard time managing my pain through divorce. I was depressed, and sometimes it was hard to get out of bed, let alone make decisions for my daughter and my future, and hope they were good ones. This is why I am so passionate about what I do. I don't want you to feel this way. I want to bring you hope! So, now I help you navigate the divorce process, make good decisions, and successfully move into the next chapter. I didn't know about Certified Divorce Coaches®(CDC®) until after my divorce, and I especially didn't know about Certified Divorce Financial Analysts ®(CDFA®). If I had, I would have hired both because I now see the value of a CDFA® and a CDC®. I mesh my training and support you on your journey through divorce and beyond. I am your cheerleader, your voice of reason, your confidant, your very own personal divorce guide!

I see my clients come through with all kinds of emotions. It helps me to understand that they are grieving and that I grieved, too. You are mourning the loss of your marriage and even, for some, the loss of a friend and partner with whom you shared many memories, the person you turned to and had intellectual conversations with, and more. You have history!

A Door That Once Linked Our Destinies

In the stillness, your heart holds onto memories like footsteps reverberating in an empty hallway. There is a door that once linked your lives together. Grief is the key that unlocks this door. This door is not ordinary, as it reminds you of your loss and brings some sense of familiarity. There is a threshold between what once was and what will be. As you step over this threshold, you leave behind the warmth and understanding; as the sunlight peeks through, you will breathe in fresh air and taste freedom mixed with your salty tears.

When someone passes away, people tend to offer sympathy and support. They check up on you, bring you meals, and send you flowers. However, when you go through a divorce, there isn't much consolation or comfort that others can provide. Could it be because they don't know what to say? It's possible.

The truth is that the grief following the end of a marriage can feel as intense as the grief felt after the death of a loved one. It can be confusing because, in both cases, the loss is profound. Perhaps this is because, with death, the person who is gone still loved you, whereas, in the case of a divorce, the spouse chooses to leave on their own. This cuts deep!

Grief comes in many colors and changes daily and sometimes hour by hour. People tend to want to rush through grief, as it hurts, and they especially don't want to hang on to loss, but grief is hanging onto love—that is why you feel it so much. Rushing through it does not make it disappear; it will show itself differently and potentially lead to short-circuiting. A confusing array of emotions is typical, but the good news is that these emotions will not always be this intense.

There is a power to being with people who get it, as we cannot process this grief alone. Often, our well-meaning friends have difficulty supporting us effectively. When you're going through a divorce, it's common for your friends and family to react emotionally to the situation. Someone who has experienced a divorce themselves may find your situation triggering, or perhaps they may feel a sense of loss as your spouse may be an integral part of their life, too, or they may want to offer protection to you during this difficult time.

It's important to seek outside, unbiased support to help you process your feelings of pain, anger, and possibly resentment. It may help you work through the emotional challenges of divorce and move you forward with certainty.

Grief is a journey through sorrow that is unique to everyone. It serves as a reminder of the presence of love, even if it has transformed. No one can experience it for you, but others can walk with you along this path.

These feelings of grief may ebb and flow throughout the process. Sometimes, we may fall back just when life is moving forward. Don't despair; keep putting one foot before the other, and soon you'll walk out the door. Then, there will come a time when you finally feel it. Hope! That's when you know you are almost on the other side.

Some of the grief phases in divorce are:

1. Shock, Denial, and Rejection

2. Fear and Anger

3. Negotiating and Bargaining

4. Guilt and Depression

5. Acknowledgment

Shock, Denial, and Rejection

At this time, you may refuse to accept that divorce is on your doorstep, or you may even be trying to avoid the pain of what reality is bringing you that you are yet ready to conquer. Even if you saw the divorce coming for years, it can be a shock when it finally arrives. And the trauma that happens when it comes out of the blue can be devastating. What can make it worse is when others make judgments about your actions and decisions before or after divorce.

While you may agree to go through a divorce, emotionally, you cannot come to terms with the fact that the relationship is coming to an end. Denial can be a defense mechanism that can shut you down emotionally and gradually ease you into the rest of the grieving process. It may spare you from feeling the full impact all at once. During this time, you may exhibit confusion and a reluctance to accept the truth, and you may even detach from the rest of the world and shut down.

Reflection Points

- How do you feel right now?

- How would you like to feel?

Fear and Anger

Fear and anger can last throughout the process, fading and diminishing. Anger can cause people to respond in unhealthy ways that they may feel are perfectly acceptable, especially if the other person caused them harm. Intense rage can surface, as well as resentment towards the soon-to-be ex-spouse or the situation. Some may target their rage at people, places, or things that get caught in the crosshairs, such as children, mediators, or attorneys. Emotional outbursts are an outlet for displaying the pain and frustration with ending the relationship. You may wonder who this new person is looking back at you in the mirror or even if this is the same person that you married. This juncture leads to feelings of betrayal, injustice, and profound loss. Malicious words and actions are not helpful; instead, it is essential not to suppress these emotions but to display them healthily so you can move beyond and ultimately overcome.

For many, it can be excruciating to realize that the divorce is happening, even though they still have deep feelings for their spouse. Even if their spouse had an affair, betrayed their trust, or hurt them deeply, they may still feel love for them. I get this! Be honest with yourself about how you are feeling! Whether it is a loss of plans, the loss of your conversations, or the loss of your confidant and best friend. Acknowledge it.

Reflection Points

- What will you do with the energy that anger provides?

- What are the losses you are feeling?

- How will your love look different than it did before?

Negotiating and Bargaining

A person may find themselves compromising to save the relationship or avoiding the consequences of divorce. It may lead to feelings of guilt, fear, anxiety, and blame. For me, I wanted to know what I could have done better. I asked, "How could I have been a better wife or mother?" I desperately wanted to communicate how the breakdown happened and what my part was that I could take accountability for. I continually asked myself "if only" questions and ruminated over different scenarios. I would have begged (to my dismay, I think I may have done this), borrowed, and stolen to negotiate an end to all the pain and consequences I was starting to feel around the end of my marriage.

Guilt and Depression

Even with the best support, a person may feel hopeless, sad, guilty, or lonely and lose interest in life. During this time, they may feel guilty about divorcing their spouse or the pain they are causing others. They also may feel depressed, unable to face the world or make reasonable decisions. Depression can manifest in feelings of helplessness, hopelessness, and a decline in energy and interest in activities that once brought joy. While some sadness and depression are expected, these feelings should diminish over time. If you are finding it difficult to move beyond these feelings of sadness, getting some professional help from a mental health professional is paramount.

Acknowledgment

Acknowledgment is when a person comes to terms with divorce and moves on with their life. I use the word acknowledgment rather than acceptance because you may never truly accept if you did not initiate the divorce, but you can make space for this new reality. In this, grief transforms. It becomes a companion, not an adversary. It whispers secrets of resilience, reminding you that endings are also beginnings. The door opens wide, beckoning you to enter a new chapter where you can redefine yourself by taking one step at a time. It can be a massive relief for those who finally experience this phase. They can now approach life with a clear head and move on. Over time, the fog of grief will dissipate, and you will realize that you will be okay. Although you may never fully come to terms with the end of your marriage and the closure you would have wanted, signs that you have reached this point include adapting and coping with the change. It is essential to remind yourself during times of grief that it does not have to limit or define you. It can be a doorway—an opening to embrace the unknown. We can, at this point, learn to live with it. And, sometimes, we thrive despite it.

In most cases, one partner may have come to terms with the end of the relationship before the other. If you feel that your partner is surprised by the news and you have already emotionally moved on, they might be reluctant to proceed with the divorce. That means they are in the initial phases of grief for their marriage, and they may need a little time to work through their emotions.

Hopefully, this information will provide insight and allow you to navigate through the phases of grief with greater awareness and compassion for yourself and your partner.

Reflection Points

- What insights have you gained from looking at your pain?

- How can your pain be used to help you through the divorce process?

Opposite Sides of the Door

Are we on a break? Like Ross and Rachel, this might get complicated, and there are mixed reviews on whether it is best to separate first, even if divorce is likely on your doorstep. This approach can allow you to live on opposite sides of the door, each in their own world.

The advantage doesn't come precisely from parting and living separately but from allowing enough time to prepare. Just like it takes time to decide to get married and plan a wedding, ending a marriage should also be approached with careful consideration. This may allow each partner enough time to prepare themselves emotionally, physically, and realistically.

Divorce involves complex financial considerations. Rushing into divorce without adequate preparation could be harmful to your future. Giving yourself time allows for a smoother transition and better decision-making.

One of my survey respondents shared that before she proceeded with divorce, she separated from her husband for about six months. After experiencing mistreatment in her marriage, she lacked confidence and self-belief. However, separating from her husband gave her ample time to prepare for the future and gather the courage to initiate the divorce.

This period can give you emotional freedom and clarity, enabling you to move forward with strength.

Reflection Points

- Do you still have feelings for your partner?

- What do you hope divorce will achieve?

Expressing the Door to My Heart

If you are the one contemplating, there comes a time when you must muster up the courage and strength to tell them. There is no tried-and-true method for telling them, so it is vital to think of how the two of you communicate and devise a plan that works for you.

Now that you have done some self-reflection and preparation and feel confident about the path forward, let's explore a few tips that may help you have a favorable outcome when letting them know you want a divorce.

1. **Compose a clear and concise message** and be prepared for how your spouse will react. Being prepared for this conversation will help reduce some of your nervousness. Going over some main points will make your talking points easier to remember in the heat of the moment. During a conversation like this, you need to contend with your emotions and your partner's. If you anticipate it being a difficult conversation, consider your spouse's questions and prepare how you may answer them. Remember, you don't need to say this word for word, but have a general idea of what you want to say and how you want to say it.

2. **Choose the right time and place** to have the conversation. It is crucial to consider the person you are speaking to. While mentioning that you would like a divorce during a fight is not unheard of, it is probably not the best route to establish success

and can lead to communication and insecurity issues with your spouse. For such vital conversations like this one, in-person might be best, but perhaps you like the privacy of a telephone conversation. If you do it in person, find a public and neutral location, such as a park, café, or other quiet spot. No matter where you decide, allow your partner to soak in the information.

3. **Express your feelings** with a focus on why you made this decision. Consider what is motivating you, and make sure you express yourself thoughtfully. If you are feeling guilty about hurting them, make sure you reaffirm why it needs to happen. Try to avoid any blame at this time. Use "I" statements, such as "I feel this divorce is best for us," instead of "You are always angry, and it does not work anymore." Animosity will only start you off on the wrong foot.

4. **Sticking with the facts** and keeping it simple will keep the conversation focused on what is most important.

5. **Have patience and listen** to your spouse, too! After you have expressed yourself, allow them to do the same.

Ultimately, the goal is to have a dignified conversation. Divorce can be difficult, and having open and honest communication is essential. This is your first step down the divorce path together; try to start on the right foot. Try hard to remain calm and respectful. Planning and utilizing some of these tips can help the conversation flow smoothly.

"Walls keep everyone out.

Boundaries teach people where the door is."

– Mark Groves

6

Thriving is the Goal

THE UNIVERSE HAS A MASTER KEY TO ALL DOORS

Y ou want it over and done. I get it. Our journey is guided by a greater plan or order that unlocks doors at the right time. Experiencing stress and trauma can impact our ability to make sound decisions. Major life events like divorce can leave individuals feeling vulnerable and make them susceptible to being taken advantage of. Rushing through divorce proceedings without seeking legal advice, signing documents without fully understanding them, and inaccurately valuing or characterizing marital assets are all potential risks. In some cases, individuals may be so desperate to escape an unhealthy marriage that they are willing to walk away from the assets to which they are entitled. Conversely, others may remain in unhappy marriages for financial reasons.

Everything you purchase during your marriage, even if only in one spouse's name, is generally considered marital or community property. Gifts, inheritance, and assets listed separately in a prenuptial agreement are non-marital property.

Remember that it's not about being kind during this trying time. Instead, it's about taking the time to ensure that you and your children get what you deserve. Your children deserve to have a comfortable life and not worry about finances when spending time with you. By acting now, you're securing a better future for yourself and your children. Your future self will thank you for trying to get everything you deserve.

Even in the best scenarios, these challenging times can be emotionally draining. Naturally, I am an introvert, but I went further inside during my divorce. I built some more walls to protect myself, not to shut others out, but to safeguard what remains from further pain. I am also a very emotional person. Even when I try to feel nothing, I feel all of it. I made it through on too much binge eating and Friends re-runs. Chandler Bing made me laugh at a time when I felt like I may never laugh again. I was usually a book reader, but I was having difficulty focusing.

In such trying times, finding reliable sources of guidance and support is essential, even if it is binge-watching shows, cuddling with your dog, and eating dinner in bed.

Here are tips and tricks for surviving and thriving in a divorce.

Seek help early

Starting as early as possible gives you an advantage by helping you make well-informed decisions and collecting the necessary documentation for your case. By understanding the scenario comprehensively and being aware of your rights, you will be better prepared to handle any challenging situations that may arise during this process.

If you are divorcing someone manipulative and controlling, it can prove to be very difficult. Start working with a divorce coach as soon as possible to develop a strategy to prevent their behaviors from affecting your emotions. This can make a massive difference in the long run. Be prepared for their love bombing, attempts to take pity on you, the blame they may throw at you, and gaslighting. This may also help you with the result your attorney and mediator can achieve.

Opening the Door to Financial Freedom

Divorce can have a significant impact on your finances. Although marital status doesn't appear on your credit report, divorce can still affect your financial situation, including your ability to make timely payments. Managing your debt during a divorce can be incredibly challenging, and avoiding any negative impact on your credit score is essential. One good strategy, if the option is available, is to pay off joint debts through negotiations during your divorce agreement. You can use savings, retirement funds, or proceeds from selling joint assets to ensure the outcome is fair and just for everyone involved. By carefully managing your debt and financial picture, you can reduce stress and start fresh in your next chapter.

Speaking with a Certified Divorce Financial Analyst® (CDFA®) is essential to make sound financial decisions. You will understand the implications of decisions on your taxes, retirement plans, and other critical aspects of your financial well-being. Doing so allows you to set yourself up for a more secure and organized future after divorce.

To find a Certified Divorce Financial Analyst® near you, go to www .institutedfa.com

Emotional Housekeeping

Your emotions can impact your decision-making, relationships, and overall well-being. Like tidying up your physical space, caring for your feelings ensures a harmonious inner self environment. You are the curator of your emotional home; that's why learning how to keep your emotions in check is crucial. As much as you may want to vent your frustrations to your attorney, that is not their role. You are spending money for them to advocate for you, not to deal with your emotional welfare. Instead, try confiding in close friends, family members, or professionals like a therapist, divorce coach, or support group to help you manage these emotions. Practicing inner peace and resilience is essential, especially when facing challenges. Focus on what's within your control and accept what you cannot change. Prioritize where you invest your energy, as the energy tank may be low during these times. Choose your battles wisely. This will keep the expenses down and resiliency up. Creating an emotional support system ensures you don't mix your emotions with crucial decision-making processes during turbulent times.

Protect Your Parameter

It's essential to be cautious when communicating with your ex-partner. Recognize potential conflict points or situations where boundaries might be tested. This could include communication frequency, access to shared spaces, or financial matters.

Responding to every accusation they make can only make things worse. It's best to only respond to important texts or emails. Remember that your ex-partner no longer has an all-access pass to you, so there's no need to engage with them regularly. Your time and energy are valuable, and it's essential to protect them now.

Protecting your personal space, prioritizing your well-being, and sticking to your set boundaries is essential. Establish clear consequences for any actions that cross those lines and communicate respectfully. Be honest about what you can tolerate and what feels uncomfortable. If your spouse exceeds your limit, be firm in enforcing the consequences. This is your chance to teach them how you expect to be treated from now on. Choosing not to argue with those who consistently misunderstand you is an act of self-care and self-respect.

If you fail to set clear boundaries, you risk being taken advantage of. I understand this can require self-discipline. During this challenging time, it is essential to stick to your boundaries to protect your emotional health and create a smoother transition.

Reflection Points

- What are the triggering areas that cause conflict between you and your spouse?

- What can you tolerate?

- What is crossing the line for you?

- How can you communicate this information to your spouse?

- What are some boundaries you would like to establish?

- What are clear consequences you can establish to protect your boundaries?

"Two roads diverged in a wood, and I—

I took the one less traveled by,

And that has made all the difference."

— **Robert Frost**

7

Responding to Divorce

WHO CAN IT BE KNOCKING AT MY DOOR?

P lease go away, I don't want you! Could this be happening? No, I
do not want you on my doorstep, and I especially do not want you
to come through that door. If I ignore it, will it go away? I mean, who
comes to a house unannounced these days anyway? Oh no, the door is
opening.

C-R-E-A-K

C-R-E-A-K

C-R-E-A-K

Did I forget to lock that darn door?

SLAM!

Phew! Problem averted!

Or is it? Maybe if I turn off all the lights and barricade myself in
here, I can avoid anyone or anything coming through that door ... FOR
GOOD!

Wait. How are they getting through my door? I wore my protective
suit of armor and created some barriers so no one could break through!

Now, I feel defenseless.

It was inevitable.

I knew it, but I didn't want to face it—not here, not now.

I could have told you many years ago that it would happen. That was a
way to protect myself, always expecting the worst so that if it did happen,

it would hurt less. That didn't prevent my hurt because it still made me feel the PAIN.

I felt it and saw those red flags with my very own eyes.

Did I want better for myself? Of course!

Did I want to get a divorce? Hell no!

We had built a life with a beautiful daughter, a fantastic family, great friends, and a community we loved. We had hopes and dreams for the future—all shattered by the simple phrase, "I want a divorce!"

That phrase is bewildering. I don't even think I heard it; maybe it was never uttered, but my heart received it and detected its presence. I remember bringing the subject up as I could not stand living like this anymore. Some details of what happened after are blurry, but that moment is precise as if it had happened yesterday.

I was at work, and my work friends were discussing their significant others, all the things they were good at, how much they felt loved, and how much each loved them back. I thought, "How come I don't have that?" I couldn't even contribute to the conversation. I just sat silently. That's when it hit me like a load of bricks! The moment I decided I had to act. I knew he wasn't happy, and if I waited for him, the words may never come, and this may be a long, distant road. My dad had just passed away a few months ago, and I didn't think I could handle any more grief. There was a pit in my stomach as I dreaded the inevitable. Nonetheless, I needed to know.

So, I called him on the way home and said: "We need to talk."

I have heard that knowing when to walk away is wisdom, being able to leave is courageous, and walking away with your head held high is dignity. That's what I wanted, to go while I still had my dignity.

When we arrived home, we sensed the impending conversation. It wasn't a formal discussion; this one occurred as we stood around the dining table. It could be because we both recognized the need for a way out. Regardless, I was aware of what was coming, and my anxiety was through the roof. It was the beginning of the end.

In the months leading up to my dad's passing from Alzheimer's, my husband was my rock. I am so grateful for his unwavering support during that difficult time, as I don't think I could have made it through without him. However, his love and care gave me hope for the future, which made the loss of my father slightly easier to bear.

One of a person's most painful experiences is feeling significant to someone only to have that taken away. It's like being on a rollercoaster, going up one minute and down the next. This kind of emotional whiplash can be confusing and hurtful.

To make matters worse, you're expected to act like nothing happened; you have to be a mom still, go to work, and live your life, even though you're struggling to cope with the pain. Losing both my father's love and my husband's support was double the grief I had to bear ALL AT ONCE.

I vowed not to retaliate and hurt him, knowing it wouldn't bring me relief or resolve. I pondered over what I would gain from hurting him, and my conclusion was that it would only make me feel worse about myself and complicate things further. My goal was to be proud of myself and make my dad proud, who always taught me that revenge is never the answer, no matter how much someone has hurt you. Additionally, I wanted to be a role model for my daughter. She deserved better than that, and I knew I could do it FOR HER!

It would have been much easier to respond with anger and resentment because that is what I felt. Staying calm and composed requires excellent strength and resilience. My father taught me to respond with kindness, compassion, and moral integrity and to rise above negative feelings, just like a proper penguin would. He taught me the value of handling situations in this manner.

Although I felt the emotion, my goal was to express it constructively. Yes, I made quick stabs during mediation and at our house closing, but nothing destructive—merely flesh wounds.

Looking back, I am full of pride in how I reacted. I know my dad is, too! In the heat of the moment, I could have made waves, but I chose the road less traveled.

Divorce does not determine your worth. It's a chapter of your life that cannot be skipped, no matter how much you want to. Although you may not enjoy every part of your story, going through tough times can help you appreciate the good things life brings. Sometimes, our lives must be changed and rearranged to get us where we are meant to be. I wouldn't have been here to help you if I hadn't gone through all this. I am grateful now for all the shaking and displacing. Destiny knocks on our doors like an unwelcome visitor, inviting us to step into new chapters of our lives.

Unlocking the Door to Your Soul

When your spouse asks for a divorce, it is hard to keep your emotions in check. Believe me. I know the first thing you will want to do is possibly beg, spout venomously, or even slam the door hard. If you're going to save your marriage, avoid sabotaging this outcome by acting angry or vengeful. Often, these actions result from feeling discouraged or hopeless, but this usually causes the reverse of what you desire.

Consider my mediation client, Ralph. Initially, Ralph made a wise choice by opting for mediation to proceed with the divorce. However, he took several opportunities to disrupt the progression during the process. One particular thing that stood out to me was his contradictory attitude. He expressed a desire to save the marriage in one instance but then spoke negatively about his wife and her family in the next. While I tried to understand that his words were driven by anger, there is never a justification for speaking to someone in such a disrespectful manner. His behavior made his wife want to run away instead of perhaps staying to work things out. His approach ultimately backfired.

Reflection Points

- Do you want to convince your spouse to go to marriage counseling? If they agree, what are the steps to ensure smooth conversations?

- How can you frame the next steps for success?

- What action can you take to feel connected with your wants and needs?

- What could you do to remain cheerful during this time?

- What do you need to do to look forward to your next chapter?

- How can you take care of yourself during this challenging time?

- What can you do to make sure you don't take your anger out on your spouse and others?

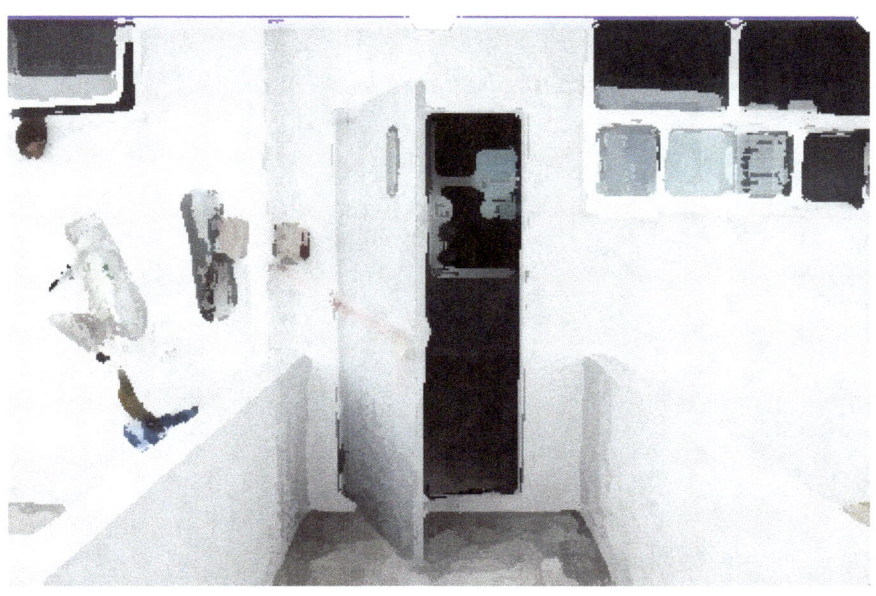

"I can see no way out but through."

– Robert Frost

8

Getting a Divorce

IF OPPORTUNITY DOESN'T KNOCK, BUILD A DOOR

There are multiple approaches to ending your marriage. The good news is that you don't have to go through lawyers; several options are less emotionally and financially draining than this adversarial process. Of course, there is room for lawyers in each approach, meaning you should always have independent counsel review your agreement before proceeding to court. Review counsel reviews the agreement on your behalf.

Divorce is never going to be a pleasant experience. Still, if you can look back knowing you handled it with dignity and were respectful towards your ex-partner and your more comprehensive network of loved ones, it'll be a far less painful memory.

Conventional Method

In this traditional divorce path, each spouse hires an attorney. The first step in most states is to file a petition indicating that you plan to end the marriage. The hired attorneys will advocate for their respective parties, taking sides. Lawyers can help represent your interests if you and your spouse disagree. They can also help navigate the legal system.

This conventional legal pathway can benefit individuals who require an advocate, especially when dealing with a manipulator or if your spouse provokes you. Advocates are here to help and support you. However, it is essential to note that their services can come with a high cost, as they charge by the hour with no limit. On average, a divorce in the US costs $9,969, with the price increasing by an average of 39% when children are involved. This can often strain the financial resources of families going through a difficult time and cause unnecessary harm to those already in turmoil. Sometimes, this method can involve scheduling delays, making the processes longer and more frustrating, taking months or even years. I have even seen my clients deal with a spouse who fires their attorney for no reason except to delay the process. Conflict may arise through exchanges between opposing attorneys and their clients. Additionally, it can deprive parents of the opportunity to make decisions regarding their family's future.

It is best to have a list of questions prepared to ask a potential divorce attorney.

1. **Ask about their experience.** What kind of experience does the attorney have, is it the central part of their practice, and is their experience in matters similar to your case?

2. **Ask for advice that they would give you.** This gives you insight into how they work and what kind of person they are.

3. **Ask about your options.** Would alternative dispute resolutions like mediation or collaborative law suit my situation?

4. **Ask how the two of you will communicate.** This will help determine how you will keep one another informed. Understand the frequency and method of communication.

5. **Determine expectations.** What do they expect from you as a client?

6. **Learn about their fee structure**. Understanding their practice will be helpful since every attorney bills clients differently.

7. **How will you work together** to get the most value from your hard-earned money?

Make sure to interview a few attorneys. Find someone who fits nicely with you, with whom you feel confident, and who understands your circumstances and motivation.

Achieve It Independently

You can create a doorway by yourself using the Pro Se Divorce method. Pro Se is a Latin term meaning "advocating for oneself" or "on behalf of oneself." This is also known as the DIY (Do It Yourself) method. As a couple, you each represent yourself in court by filing the required paperwork. Most states have online paperwork you can print out, making it much more manageable. This method is usually used by couples who want to save money and time. It is most effective for simple and uncomplicated settlements, where both parties agree and no children are involved.

This approach necessitates strong communication skills and a willingness to compromise. Stress and trauma can impact our decision-making, and individuals undergoing major life events such as divorce are susceptible to being taken advantage of. Hurrying through a divorce without sufficient guidance, signing documents without understanding them, and inaccurately assessing and categorizing marital assets all pose potential risks. Some individuals are so eager to escape an unhealthy marriage that they are willing to relinquish entitlement to assets. Don't let this happen to you.

Those who are easily influenced should consider an Alternative Dispute Resolution (ADR) method, such as collaboration or mediation. With proper guidance, it can be easier to understand what one deserves and navigate the complexities of the divorce paperwork and proceedings.

Go, Team, Go!

Collaborative Divorce Law utilizes a "Team" approach to divorcing. This Alternative Dispute Resolution (ADR) method emphasizes cooperation rather than litigation. Each spouse hires an attorney and vows to work together to resolve divorce-related issues. This team approach typically involves hiring a Financial Neutral and a Divorce Coach or Therapist to assist in the process. This process allows for managing the couple's unique legal, financial, and emotional aspects. This approach tends to be more adversarial than mediation, with the primary goal of avoiding lengthy, drawn-out courtroom battles.

In summary, this collaborative, team approach can save time, money, and anxiety when a settlement can be reached.

Hit the High Road

A mediator is critical in helping you navigate the details of your divorce. They facilitate discussions about asset division, childcare agreements, and other aspects of the marriage. Once all elements are accounted for, they typically draft an agreement for both parties to sign. This process is impartial, voluntary, and confidential, and most importantly, it empowers the involved parties to make the final decisions rather than attorneys or judges.

Couples usually set the pace of how quickly the marriage can be dissolved as they determine how often they meet with the mediator and how quickly they file the agreement. Couples usually spend 80 to 90 percent less time and money utilizing a mediator over an alternative approach and typically have comparable outcomes with more informed decision-making.

You may ask, how can a Mediator be truly neutral? I can only speak for myself, but I can't help it. I have compassion for both parties going through this process, whether they are initiating it or finding themselves in this situation. You may think it is because I have been on both sides, possibly. Of course, I encounter similar situations, but most situations are unique.

I have always tried to be impartial and unbiased, perhaps even to a fault. I prefer avoiding drama and looking for good in people and situations. However, my daughter thinks my tendency to talk to random strangers is not a good trait, as she worries about my safety. I do it because I want to spread joy and kindness. Random acts of kindness, like complimenting someone or smiling at a stranger, are always what I strive for. Kindness can go a long way, and having a soft heart in a cruel world is courage, not weakness. This world harnesses too much negativity, and we all need more love. It is not why I went into mediation, but maybe it makes me a better mediator.

I utilized the mediation process to get my divorce. I felt very alone. My spouse, who I had always relied on for help making decisions, was no longer available to me. Not to mention, he is an attorney. He's not a divorce attorney, but still … it was scary! I felt he knew more about the process and how to negotiate effectively. I wasn't giving myself enough credit, but it felt personal and potentially devastating. I wished someone was by my side to help me make good decisions. I found it difficult to focus during the mediation process due to my foggy brain, and some days, I didn't want to get out of bed, let alone make decisions. I knew the decisions made during this time would significantly impact my future and my daughter's. This is why I created the Personal Divorce Guide and became a mediator.

Mediation has become more popular in the past few years. It is a lower-cost alternative that takes less time. Some states even offer incentives for using mediation, such as waiving waiting periods or not requiring one spouse to be served by a Marshall.

Should everyone go through mediation? No. If there is any abuse—physical, emotional, and even financial—I would suggest you get someone to advocate for you; that is the lawyer's job! But, if you feel that you and your spouse can make decisions together, amicability, there is no harm in trying. What have you got to lose? Even if you have spent some money and time with the mediator, you will have your financials in place and maybe have made a few decisions, so nothing is wasted.

The question of the day is, "What does amicably even mean"? According to Merriam-Webster Dictionary, Amicably is characterized by friendly and peaceable[1]. Does it mean you must be kind or not upset about the divorce? No, it doesn't. It means that you are willing to work together. You don't have to be thrilled with the situation; I know I wasn't, but I knew I wanted what was best for my daughter, and that wasn't litigation. I wanted a scenario that was peaceful and calm. It's truly a state of mind that you need to embrace!

The most significant benefit of utilizing mediation is for the children as it helps parents successfully transition into the next chapter and co-parent effectively.

Divorce documents put together by a mediator have a higher compliance rate because both spouses have agency when deciding on the agreement. In other words, both parties are more likely to follow the divorce agreement because they fully participated in putting it together.

Here are a few tips to make mediation successful:

1. **Be prepared.** The mediator will likely ask you to gather documents to show your financial situation and prepare court documentation. The information collected will support and verify your situation. Having this information ready can speed up the process and make it more efficient.

2. **Be respectful**. Try to be courteous and willing to understand your partner's feelings and perspectives, no matter what caused the situation in the first place. Avoiding blame or personal attacks can sidetrack you and harm the process and goal of mediation. Respecting your spouse and the mediator helps create trust and moves the process forward.

---

1. https://www.merriam-webster.com/dictionary/amicable

3. **<u>Be flexible.</u>** During mediation, you seek a fair agreement for all parties. It is essential to be open to different options. Having an open mind and exploring different scenarios allows everyone to find a resolution together.

4. **<u>Be patient.</u>** Yes, mediation tends to be quicker, but it still takes a little time to pull everything together and agree. I look at it like building a puzzle. You must have all the pieces to create the puzzle and reach an agreement. You will surely get there if you invest the time and effort needed to reach a resolution!

One of the drawbacks of mediation is that you have to advocate for yourself, which can be challenging as negotiation skills are essential. If you're feeling nervous about this, it's helpful to hire a CDFA® or a divorce coach to assist you in preparing for your sessions, equipping you with negotiation strategies, and devising a settlement plan.

For example, my client, Sally, sought my help before beginning the divorce process. She was concerned about her financial situation post-divorce. We worked together to review her finances, determine a fair settlement for her and her family, and develop a plan for moving forward. We also discussed the most suitable process for her situation. We prepared for sessions and discussed effective negotiation strategies tailored to her circumstances as she proceeded. She expressed gratitude for having my support and guidance throughout the process.

No matter which way you decide to get divorced, please don't self-sacrifice and give away your future. Protect your future and get what you deserve.

Reflection Points

- What is the best method for divorcing based on your specific circumstances?

- What are the advantages of utilizing this approach in your situation?

- What are the disadvantages for you?

"Before anything else, preparation is the key to success."

-Alexander Graham Bell

9

Preparing and Organizing

The Doors of Wisdom are Never Shut

A re you ready to step through the door? No matter what led to your divorce or what your spouse did, your most brilliant strategy is to be organized, respectful, and get through as fast as you can while making intelligent, long-term decisions. Something I read that I wish I had seen before I went through my divorce is this, "You need to make many decisions while going through the process, so make choices based on the life you're creating, not the one you're leaving behind." This spoke to me. What this meant to me is that there are so many decisions you will need to make in divorce; don't let resentment, fear, or anger guide you. Granted, no choice will ever be perfect, but if you can make them based on where you want to be, you will cross the right threshold.

One spouse usually manages the family's finances. They handle the investment opportunities, pay the bills, and balance the checking and savings accounts. They know what they owe and what they own. Too often, the other partner is not aware. Now is the time to become informed. Gather your statements, run your credit reports, and organize your financial picture as early as possible before a divorce arrives at your door.

I heard this from one of my colleagues: "Finances have a way of working themselves out!" Is it going to be easy? NO! Go in with your eyes wide open! I firmly believe in doing your due diligence and becoming as educated and informed as possible—with everything, especially divorce! I know you are asking, but how do I do this, Shell? First, don't just jump in and retain the first mediator or attorney that comes your way— that is what I call "doing the penguin plunge!" Jumping in the water, feet first, without dipping your toe in to get a temperature reading. Once you hit the water, you will get the shock of your life! Don't start swimming; there will be plenty of time for that; take this stretch to prepare for the road ahead. This is a marathon, not a sprint!

I know you want this done. You probably feel you've waited long enough already. However, this race is unique, unlike anything you have encountered before, and each participant will have their own experience. Please don't pay the registration fees before you are sure that you can make it to the finish line successfully. Ensure you know the course and what to expect, and make a tried and true training plan! The training plan should allow you to start slowly and build strength and resiliency. Then, when you feel you are good and ready, sign up and let the games begin!

The best way forward is to plan and have some strategies in place.

Rainy Days, Sunny Savings

Doesn't having money make you feel more empowered and less fearful? Ensure you have cash in an individual account that only you can access. It is common for couples to merge all their accounts, but each needs access to some funds just in case the relationship goes south, and your spouse closes the door on the cash vault.

My suggestion is to put money aside slowly to avoid alarms and ensure account statements are sent to a safe address. A P.O. box or no paper statements is a great idea (only available online).

This DOES NOT mean hiding money. Please don't do that. You will disclose this account when the time comes. It just means you have cash available to use at your discretion. Whether it is to hire a team of professionals, allow you some self-care when you need it most, or give you some peace of mind.

It's essential to have an easily accessible rainy-day fund. You should save enough money to cover three to six months of basic living expenses. Keep this money in a separate account that is highly liquid, which means you can access it quickly when needed. Keep this fund separate from your other investments and everyday money.

Opening a bank account is especially important if you're attempting to leave an abusive relationship. You don't want your former partner withholding funds from you as a way of controlling you.

I had a client whose husband changed their health plan to a high deductible plan in the middle of their divorce, so she had substantial unexpected health care expenses that she wasn't aware would happen. Having a buffer for these surprises is essential! Accumulated funds would have come in handy for her!

Your account will also give you a jumpstart on separating yourself from your spouse. It's hard to disentangle yourself from your spouse financially, but this is a significant first step.

I am grateful that I set up my rainy-day fund when divorce was on my doorstep. I always maintained a separate account outside my usual checking and savings accounts. My father taught me how to save money effectively, and he told me that "it is much easier to save when you don't feel it in your pocket." This account should have a competitive interest rate, no monthly maintenance fees, and no minimum balance requirement, like Capital One's Performance Savings account.[1] Whenever I received my paycheck, an automatic $25 would go into this account for safekeeping. Though it might not seem like much, it adds up over time. It feels fantastic to have a substantial amount in a safety net ready to catch you if you ever fall.

In today's world, transferring money from one bank to another has become very accessible. Although it may seem easy, I suggest that you avoid using it. My Ally savings account takes three days to transfer, and it's been hard enough to keep me from being impulsive and using it. It's essential to resist the urge. You may be able to add to this by not getting

---

1. I am not receiving a commission for this endorsement; I just like them.

an ATM card for the new bank account and not setting up the ability to transfer to the checking account you use for daily purchases. This may help you avoid making impulsive decisions and keep you on track toward achieving your goals.

Avoid using a Certificate of Deposit (CD) for your emergency savings account. Although CDs typically offer higher interest rates, they require you to keep your money locked in for a specific term. It may be problematic if it is urgent to access your funds. Additionally, CDs often require a lump sum upfront, which means you are not able to add additional funds to the account until it matures

It is advisable to refrain from using an account solely dependent on the stock market, such as a mutual fund, for your emergency fund. While offering potential growth, mutual funds are less liquid than cash or savings accounts. They are subject to market fluctuations and exposed to market risk. Imagine needing these funds during a market downturn. In an emergency, there might be more feasible options than waiting for the sale of mutual fund shares to complete.

Moreover, selling mutual fund shares can lead to capital gains taxes. You may owe taxes on any gains when you withdraw from a taxable investment account. In contrast, a dedicated emergency fund in a regular savings account doesn't have tax implications when you access it. These funds are ideal, providing a sense of security and preparedness.

Reflection Points

- Do you have a checking/savings account with money you can utilize?

- If not, how can you open one and start accumulating a balance?

Balancing Debts, Counting Blessings

Be proactive in gathering your financial information. It may save you a lot of legal fees, as you will minimize the time your attorney or mediator asks for documents. This will also give you a clearer picture of your financial situation, empowering you to take control of your financial future.

The first order of business in divorce is usually gathering the finances. So, get those ducks in a row now, and you will be a step up in the process.

It's essential to prioritize your finances. Though dealing with financial matters can be tedious, it's crucial for maintaining your credibility. Therefore, it's best not to procrastinate but to dedicate time and effort to ensure accuracy.

This part of the process can feel daunting, especially if you need access to the information. But please don't fret; this is simply an inventory of items. If something is unavailable, make a note and discuss it with your Certified Divorce Financial Analyst®. You can work together to determine the best way to access the documentation.

My Financial Document Checklist can be accessed through the QR code under the "Workbook" chapter. It will provide the most requested information, but given your unique circumstances, you might also need other information.

It will give you a snapshot of your finances in time. Therefore, if anything changes, you will know. Divorce often causes people to exhibit their worst behaviors. One thing I see people do is try to manipulate their finances during divorce. You may say, "My spouse would never do that." Many people say they don't need to prepare for the worst-case scenario, but it is too familiar to ignore. Therefore, it is crucial to cover all your bases and have a good line of defense in case something unexpected happens. It is always better to be prepared than to be devastated by the consequences of not being ready. Besides, finances are nothing you should rush through; you don't want to be under the gun when your attorney or mediator is waiting to move the process along, and you are potentially holding it up because you don't have the information readily available and need to rely on your bank or financial institution where your property is held to provide the details promptly. We all know how that goes!

Let's review what you should gather. Use the form I provided under the "Workbook" chapter to document all the information. I suggest setting up a folder to save all your statements on your computer and labeling each subfolder. If you would rather have hard copies, get an accordion folder and label each section. That way, they are readily available when your attorney, mediator, or CDFA® asks for your paperwork. If you can't secure copies, take pictures of the documents with your phone.

Real Estate (Primary Home, vacation homes, rental properties)

Estimated Value: Knowing the value of your home can help you make informed decisions about keeping or selling your home. A simple and easy way to obtain your current value is to ask a Real Estate Professional to provide you with a Competitive Market Analysis of your real estate property. They usually come at no cost to you. Don't rely on Zillow ("Zestimate"); it is not always accurate. A Zestimate is not an official appraisal but a good starting point for estimating your home value.

Mortgage Statements: A mortgage statement provides your monthly principal, interest, and escrow (insurance and property tax) payments, balance remaining, and interest rate.

Bank Statements

Include individual and joint checking, savings, money market, certificates of deposits, and anything that has liquid and near-liquid (easily and quickly converted to cash) assets.

Non-Retirement Investments

These accounts are distinct from your employer-sponsored retirement plans (like 401(k)s or 403(b)s) and individual retirement accounts (IRAs). Investors use an investment account, sometimes called a brokerage or a securities account, to buy and hold securities, such as stocks, bonds, and index funds. These can be brokerage accounts, Health Savings Accounts (HSAs) associated with your high-deductible health insurance, 529 Education Plans, or Able Accounts.

Retirement Funds

Plan sponsors manage retirement accounts and can be in one of the following types:

- Employer-sponsored plans such as 401(k), 401(a), 403(b), 457(b) or

- Personal retirement accounts such as a Traditional Individual Retirement account (IRA), a Roth IRA, or

- Business retirement accounts such as a Simplified Employee Pension (SEP)

- And, of course, something we all wish we had—pension plan(s)

Employee Stock

Employee stock allows employees to buy at a discount and partially own the company.

They can be in the form of:

- Employee stock options are the right to buy company stock at a discounted price.

- Employee Stock Ownership Plan (ESOP) is an employee benefit that gives workers ownership of the company in the form of <u>shares</u> of stock or

- Restricted Stock Account(s) are unregistered shares of stock in a company issued as part of a compensation package.

Vehicle(s)/Boats/ATVs/RVs

Estimated Value: The following websites are the best places to obtain the current value. Similar to assessing a home value, this is how to determine the value of your cars or other items.

- Vehicles on Bluebook.com,

- RVs on RVselectinc.com,

- Boats on waterbornemag.com

- Car loans and leases

Another way to gather this data is to examine similar items and their prices on popular sites.

Car Loan Statement: Do you or your spouse have a loan on your car?

Insurance (Life Insurance, Annuities, Disability Income, Long-Term Care)

Life insurance is a contract between an insurance company and a policy owner that promises to pay a benefit in the event of death; they usually come in the following forms:

- Permanent Life Insurance remains active while the person is alive as long as premiums are paid and there is a benefit upon death.

- Whole Life Insurance means it lasts your whole lifespan. It includes a cash value component, which is like a savings account.

- Universal Life Insurance also has a cash value component that earns interest. The premiums can be adjusted over time and designed with a level death benefit or an increasing death benefit.

- Variable Life Insurance allows the policyholder to invest the policy's cash value in an available separate account. It also has flexible premiums and can be designed with a level death benefit or an increasing death benefit.

- Term Life Insurance policies expire after a certain number of years.

- An Annuity is a contract with a promise to pay your regular income immediately or in the future.

- Disability Income is an insurance policy that provides income to individuals who can no longer work because of a disability.

- Long-Term Care (LTC) Insurance covers nursing home care, home health care, and personal or adult day care for individuals over 65.

Debts

Please gather all statements for any outstanding debts, whether individual or joint. This includes car loans, lease agreements, student loans, tax debts, or medical bills. Obtaining your credit report, not just your credit score, is also a good idea. You can get a free report once a year, showing all the debts reported to the credit bureaus. This is an excellent opportunity to review your credit and check for suspicious or inaccurate information. You can obtain a free report at www.annualcreditreport.com, or if you have a Credit Karma account, they provide an easy way to access it.

Hidden Treasures are Unseen Riches

There are commonly overlooked assets in a divorce. Does your spouse have a previous employer's retirement plan? Frequent flyer miles? Hobby equipment? Guns? Antiques? Do not leave a stone unturned. Doing your due diligence now will save you future angst!

Reflection Points

- What assets can you think of that need to be accounted for?

In Tax's Shadow, Ignorance Costs

Every decision comes with a tax bill, and the capital gains can be killer! This is the case with most assets, like the ocean, which is calm and beautiful on the surface. They may look "equal," but danger lurks underneath. This threat could be disguised as taxes, capital gains, inflation, or investment losses. Some retirement accounts may also impose a penalty if you take a distribution before a specific age.

Budgets: Where Dreams Can Be Accomplished

Going through a divorce can bring significant changes to your lifestyle and finances. It's vital to assess your available income and identify areas where you may need to make trade-offs to stay within your budget. You may need to cut back on certain expenses and determine what is necessary for your current situation. Creating a budget can help you figure out ways to cover your bills, save money for emergencies, and plan for your future. Regularly reviewing and adjusting your budget is crucial to meet your financial goals.

"There is no such thing as a 'broken family'

Family is family!

Marriage certificates do not determine it,

Neither do divorce papers or adoption documents.

Families are made in the heart."

- C. Joybell

10

Minimizing Impacts on Your Children

HOLD THE DOOR!

I understand that one of the most challenging aspects of divorce is the thought of spending less time with your children. You likely did everything possible to be there for them, even though it was demanding. And now, the reality of having less time with them sounds heartbreaking. I have been in your shoes and witness my clients struggling with this regularly. However, I want you to know that things will work out. By having specific parenting days, you can make the most of your time with your children while allowing the other parent to have their fair share of time with them.

Now, it is time to focus on the quality of the time you spend with them rather than the quantity. Building a plan together effectively allows you to transition from couple to co-parents successfully.

I've had clients in mediation who do not want to create a parenting plan because they believe they can keep things amicable working things out as they go along. Some have felt that their schedule is too complicated to put something in writing, fearing that they may be unable to adhere to the schedule they create together. The truth is, no schedule is too complicated. You can always find a way to make it work, even if you need to be creative.

However, conflicts may arise over schedules, holidays, and unexpected changes without a clear plan. Having these crucial conversations now and developing a well-designed co-parenting schedule can help prevent disputes and provide clear guidelines and expectations that both co-parents can adhere to.

Guiding Stars and Nurturing Choices

Parents must work together to make significant decisions concerning their children's welfare. This may include determining their education, healthcare, and other responsibilities specific to their family. With that in mind, I understand that conflict happens. The goal is always to keep disagreements at bay as much as possible, so when disputes arise, and agreements cannot be reached, it is good to establish a plan for what you will do in that situation.

If both parents cannot agree, should one parent have the authority to make significant decisions regarding the children? For example, perhaps Parent A might be responsible for education and academic choices due to their expertise in the field. At the same time, maybe Parent B might make healthcare decisions because of their familiarity with the area.

Shared Hours with Boundless Bonds

The primary goal of the parenting plan is to enable children to have consistent access to both parents, maintain stability, and minimize conflict between parents.

50/50 Parenting Plans

This is the type of plan that each parent has equal time with the children.

*Please note that the illustrations provided are for visual purposes only. They can help you create a schedule that works best for your family.

Key:

Parent A	
Parent B	

Here are several options to consider:

Alternating Weeks

This plan is simplistic. One week with Parent A, the next week with Parent B, with transitions on any day that works for the family. This split allows each parent to have a whole week with the children. The benefits are fewer transitions and more consistency for the children. However, the drawback is that each parent and child must go for a week without seeing each other.

If a week feels too long to be apart, I have had clients incorporate a mid-week visit, like dinner on Wednesdays.

*This illustration depicts that the transition will take place on Sunday.

Sunday	Monday	Tuesday	Wednesday	Thursday	Friday	Saturday

Splitting the Week

Each parent has the children for half a week. Although similar to the alternating weeks, this allows parents and children to see each other every week. This still provides consistency for the children with a few more transitions.

* This schedule ensures equal time with each parent by alternating on Tuesdays, Saturdays, and Fridays during the following transition period (2-week increments).

Sunday	Monday	Tuesday	Wednesday	Thursday	Friday	Saturday

2-2-5 Split

Parent A has two days, Parent B has two days, and alternate weekends. This arrangement offers consistency, although less than previously mentioned plans. It allows parents and children to see each other more often with some variety.

  *This illustration depicts Parent A having Mondays and Tuesdays, Parent B having Wednesdays and Thursdays, and alternating weekends. Transitions are on Mondays, Wednesdays, and Fridays, if applicable.

Sunday	Monday	Tuesday	Wednesday	Thursday	Friday	Saturday

3-4-4-3 Schedule

One parent has the child for three days, and the other has the child for four days, then switches the following week. It offers the same benefits as the 2-2-5-5 split but is split differently.

  *If applicable, this illustration depicts transitions on Tuesday, Saturday, and Wednesday.

Sunday	Monday	Tuesday	Wednesday	Thursday	Friday	Saturday

Remember that these are just examples; you should tailor your co-parenting schedule to your family's needs.

Unlocking Breaktime Bliss

A holiday and school vacation schedule is a plan that determines when each parent will spend time with the children on holidays and vacations when their school is not in session. This schedule generally takes precedence over the regular time-sharing schedule.

When creating a holiday schedule, it is crucial to consider both parents' work schedules, the children's school schedules, and any traditions or obligations.

Some popular holiday schedules have a mix of the following elements:

Odd and Even Numbered Years

Each parent has the children on an odd or even number year that is defined for the specific holiday.

Here's an example to illustrate this:

New Year's Day –
- Parent A has odd-numbered years for New Year's Day.

- Parent B has even-numbered years for New Year's Day.

Splitting the Day

Each parent has the children on certain holidays for part of the day.

Here's an example to illustrate this:

Easter –
- Parent A has the children on Easter Morning until 1 pm.

- Parent B has the children on the afternoon of Easter starting at 1 pm.

Every Year

One parent gets to enjoy time with the children every year on a specific holiday.

Here's an example to illustrate this:

Mother's Day –
- Parent A will enjoy time with the children every Mother's Day.

Dividing Vacations

Each parent has equal time with the children during their holidays from school.

Here's an example to illustrate this:

Winter Vacation –
- Parent A will enjoy time with the children at the beginning of the week.

- Parent B will enjoy time with the children at the end of the week.

When creating your holiday schedule, don't forget to consider birthdays, both yours and the children's.

Creating Harmony in Shared Chapters

Parents who are getting a divorce often have questions about child support. They want to know what it is, whether they qualify to receive it, and how it's determined. Each state uses its own method to calculate child support. I suggest looking into the specific child support calculation used in your state and understanding how it works. Keep in mind that there are various ways to apply the child support guidelines, which can help evaluate different parenting plan options and their financial impact.

Clarity Unlocks Connection. Remember to be patient and flexible when co-parenting. Expect setbacks and try to get back in sync as soon as possible. Communicate with your co-parent about potential changes or issues so everyone is on the same page. Consider including the right of first refusal in your agreement, meaning if one parent cannot spend time with the children during the agreed-upon schedule, the other parent has the first opportunity to be with the children.

Kindness Blooms, and Bridges Strengthen. Yes, it can be tempting to bash the other parent. We want to set the record straight and give our story. Oh, that would feel good to have everyone know, including our children. Even if you are the right parent and the other is behaving poorly, it does not help your child to point this out. There are sure to be many times when you want to share and feel they "need to know" that their other parent is living with his girlfriend, who could be closer to your children's age. Yes, there are a few times that I failed and gave into this temptation, significantly as my daughter grew older, but as soon as the words came out of my mouth, I saw the look on her face or even the sharp words from her mouth that I did the unspeakable. It is true that sometimes, to pull yourself from the marriage, you need to demonize the other parent. Unfortunately, anger gives you more forward momentum than sadness does.

Remember, your children are part of them. If you attack their other parent, you are attacking them!

Both parents need to promote a positive relationship between the children and the other parent. This means avoiding behaviors or language that could cause the children to become distant from the other parent. We all know that doing the right thing can be challenging, especially when it causes you to bite your tongue. However, I have witnessed too many instances of inappropriate behavior lately. Children are easily influenced; even if the other parent is not refraining from such behavior, being the bigger person is essential. You can always vent to a friend later to release your emotions.

Steadfast Steps, Unwavering Results. Maintaining a routine is essential to help your children feel safe and secure. Let's face it! We all thrive on stability and structure, especially during times like this! Of course, it will be challenging to comply with any schedule 100% of the time; as things come up, that is normal; that is life. Remaining flexible with the other parent when unexpected events arise, and accommodating travel will give your children peace of mind and ensure that everything will be okay.

Ink Your Days. A calendar displayed anywhere your children can see could be helpful. It should depict where they are going and what they are doing regularly. If they are younger, you could decorate the calendar together, using different colors or stickers for specific events or times with each parent. If they are older, update the calendar on their cell phone or keep it on a calendar you can display in the kitchen, as we all go there several times a day.

Where Heartbeats Echo. When you live in two separate dwellings and transition often, it can possibly feel like they have one foot out the door. To minimize this feeling, try to reduce the need for packing to go to each household. Have their clothing, toiletries, and items that make them feel comfortable in each home. Some things are unavoidable, like a favorite stuffed animal or textbooks, but every little bit helps.

Elegance in Simplicity. Co-parenting can be challenging, but there are apps for that! They make it easier for parents to communicate and coordinate. Talking Parent and Our Family Wizard are two such apps that offer a centralized platform for storing important information like phone numbers and vital details. Both apps also provide a shared calendar for co-parenting schedules. In addition to this, these apps have secure texting and calling features to facilitate communication between co-parents. You can also track shared parenting expenses and send or receive payments securely through these apps.

If you want something more straightforward, Google Docs can help you organize your shared expenses. Remember to keep it updated in the current time to avoid confusion.

Where Paths Converge. Make sure the location of transitioning the children from one parent to another is somewhere everyone feels safe and secure. I have many clients who were children of divorce, and they stress how important the transition location can be. I had a client whose parents lived far apart from each other. When the client was a child, her parents would meet in a McDonald's parking lot to do the "exchange." As an adult, the client has developed a severe aversion to McDonald's, and every time she passes by one, she feels a pit in her stomach.

I read Matthew Perry's memoir, *Friends, Lovers, and the Big Terrible Thing*. In it, he discusses being sent on a plane as an "Unaccompanied Minor" to see his Dad across the country. Unaccompanied Minor is a term used for kids flying without a parent. He goes on to reveal that this triggered feelings of loneliness and abandonment in his childhood and had a profound impact on his life. This is a reminder of divorce's complexities and that transitions can be challenging and emotional.

While it's natural to miss your children while they're away, something that helped me (and still does) is looking forward to reuniting again.

Keep your drawbridge up. I like the idea of avoiding asking personal questions about each other's lives. It can be challenging because sometimes you might be curious about certain things, such as whether they are dating or who they are spending time with. But sometimes, it's best not to know. Skip the drama and focus on protecting your peace. This approach can also promote independence and keep you moving forward. You have better things to do.

Reflection Points

- What visitation schedule appealed most to you and why?

- Does it work for both of your schedules?

- Is the schedule sustainable in the long run?

- Is the schedule suitable for the children?

- How can you ensure everyone will remember the schedule?

- What holiday traditions would you like to incorporate into the parenting plan?

- Are there specific holiday times you like to ensure you have the children?

- How do you envision being the best parent for your children after divorce?

- How can you and your spouse stay on good terms after the divorce?

Get Workbook Here

"The price of anything is the amount

of life you exchange for it."

– Henry David Thoreau

II

Retaining the Marital Home

SHOULD I KEEP THE DOOR?

Your house is wonderful, but it has a lot of emotional and sentimental value, which makes it a sticking point in negotiating a settlement.

Moving out before or during a divorce can be costly and complex from a financial perspective, but it's often essential for partners who feel they are in unsafe situations. Consult an attorney to ensure there are no legal ramifications to leaving the marital home. Ensure you inventory all items in your home so that you can fairly divide everything during the divorce process.

The decision to stay or leave the home you raised your family in is difficult. It may be your refuge during this difficult time, you may feel moving will disrupt your children, or you can't imagine packing and finding a new place to live right now. Make sure the reasons are realistic and not emotional. Remember that homeownership is very expensive, especially with your marital home that you supported with possibly two incomes. It is not just about paying the mortgage but also the ability to maintain the house, keep up with it, and conduct primary and minor repairs. These costs add up quickly! Ensure you assess all the costs of owning and maintaining the home before deciding who keeps it.

If both spouses purchased the home during the marriage using marital funds, it is usually considered marital property. Depending on your state, you may follow community property rules, where assets acquired during the marriage are split equally or fair and equitable, where you lean on fairness and not necessarily equality. Anything you buy during your marriage—including a house—is regarded as marital property in most states, even if it's only titled in one spouse's name. Make sure you do your due diligence on how your state views property.

Be realistic and creative with solutions.

Here are some common approaches when dividing the marital home:

Sell the home and split the proceeds. I welcome this method for my clients, as it is the most straightforward. By selling the marital home, they can relinquish debt that may burden them and start anew by renting or buying more affordable properties. This approach allows them to start fresh and move on with their lives.

We chose this approach during my divorce. I am still so grateful that we made that decision because neither of us could have afforded the property alone, as it was way too much to maintain. That home held many memories of our time together as a couple and a family; if I had kept it, it would have been a constant reminder of the dreams that were now shattered.

Buy out your spouse. Buying out the other's equity in your shared property may be possible if one spouse wants to stay in the home. Determining the equity is typically done by calculating the house's current market value (utilizing a competitive market analysis completed by a real estate professional) and then subtracting the mortgage balance. To determine the buyout amount needed, you would divide the equity by two. If both of you are on the mortgage, refinancing the home is usually recommended. However, assuming a mortgage is becoming increasingly popular, which involves taking one spouse's name off the mortgage but continuing with the interest rate. Before proceeding with refinancing, you should determine if your mortgage is assumable in divorce.

Co-own the home. A temporary solution to a costly home ownership problem could be co-owning the property. This approach typically requires both partners to keep living in and paying for all expenses related to the home, including but not limited to the mortgage, upkeep, maintenance, taxes, and insurance. Some clients have dealt with this scenario by reconfiguring the home layout, such as repurposing the basement for one party's sleeping quarters or rearranging the bedrooms to make this approach feasible.

Deferring the home sale. Consider deferring until certain circumstances are met. For example, it may be until the youngest child reaches the age of 18 or when the real estate market improves. The home would be sold then, and the proceeds would be divided accordingly.

Nesting. An increasingly popular approach is to keep the family home a stable environment for their children. Under this arrangement, the children reside in the family home. At the same time, the adults rotate in and out of the house on a predetermined schedule, living in the house during their scheduled time and having separate accommodations when they are not in the house.

I am impressed with my mediation clients who used the nesting approach. It requires excellent communication between the couple. We discussed everything from taking out the garbage and laundry to buying and preparing groceries. They took turns nesting each week and made plans to spend time with their kids during their off weeks. Since we knew it would be a temporary situation, we discussed and scheduled time for them to review the nesting arrangement and guidelines for moving forward. They were on the right track when I checked in with them recently!

Live with extended family. Having a roof over each person's head is crucial, but going from one family home to two separate houses can be costly and challenging. Because of this, one or both of you may decide to live with extended family, if possible, while alternative housing is arranged. It can save money and give you time to explore the location you want to call home.

If you are interested in keeping your home, refinancing, or assuming the mortgage, it's wise to connect with a Certified Divorce Lending Professional (CDLP). These professionals can help educate you about the mortgage planning process during divorce. To find a CDLP in your area, visit this website: www.divorcelendingprofessional.com

Changing Direction to Find the Right Door

I was adamant about finding a new house after my divorce. I know my heart wanted to do it out of spite. I was going to show him! Show him that I didn't need him, that I was financially independent, and that I was capable. I wanted the first home I saw in a neighboring town. I loved it because everything was brand new; someone had flipped it. However, the inspection uncovered many issues the seller was unwilling to correct, and the deal fell through.

Consequently, I needed to come up with an alternative solution. I ended up living with my spouse's extended family and my friends. It was the best thing I did for myself and my daughter during my divorce. It gave me time to adjust to my new normal while having a great support system to make the darker days brighter. I cannot thank them enough for opening their home and hearts to us and allowing us this opportunity. It indeed was a lifesaver, and I loved their company while going through this transition. How do you ever repay someone for giving you peace in your heart?

I finally found the perfect home during this transition period, ideal for me as a newly divorced mom and my beautiful teenage daughter. Did it matter to my ex-husband? No, he didn't seem to care much. But it mattered more to me because it showed me my true potential. It demonstrated that I was more than capable of finding a home that met our needs. It showed me that I didn't need him to make critical decisions and that I was financially independent. Most importantly, it showed me that I could create a comfortable and safe home environment for me and my daughter all on my own.

Assessing whether you can afford to keep your marital home is crucial. To make an informed decision, review the last five years of home expenses and determine the current value of your property. Using all the money you receive from child support and alimony to keep the house is tempting. Still, it's essential to consider whether it's practical and realistic for your financial situation. If you can't afford to keep the house, don't view it as a dead-end but rather as an opportunity to redirect yourself towards a better path. Remember not to let your emotions cloud your judgment when making this decision.

Reflection Points

- What happened in your past that led you to find the right door?

- What approach to your marital home makes sense for your family?

- Do you want to keep your marital home?

- Can you afford to keep your marital home?

12

Dividing Retirement Accounts

THE LAST KEY ALWAYS OPENS THE DOOR

R etirement plans are a big topic when you are going through a divorce! They are crucial in ensuring a fair agreement, achieving a clean break, and a fresh start for both parties. Conversely, besides parenting schedules, they cause the most conflict.

People are very attached to their retirement plans, including Defined Contribution, Personal Retirement, and Defined Benefit Plans. It mainly results from years of working with your blood, sweat, and tears for a company. You've worked hard—maybe giving up time with the family, holidays, or even seeing the light of day. It makes them feel a sense of ownership and entitlement. It may mean they will be willing to go to bat to keep all (or a significant portion) of the assets INTACT!

Retirement plans can be one of the most significant assets in divorce, right next to the marital home, but that marital home cannot put food on your table in retirement. These accounts may be considered community or marital property during the settlement process and must be divided appropriately. They can often be overlooked, especially if the plans were established before the marriage but have grown in value. Spouses are usually not considering retirement, and a divorce can happen years before retirement is even a thought. Having someone to assist you in considering all the necessary pieces is essential.

Retirement plans earn compound interest (interest you earn on top of what you already earned previously) and will grow even larger once your divorce is a distant memory.

Defined Contribution Plans are payroll deduction accounts that usually have a component of an employer match, such as 401(k)s, which are employer-sponsored plans; 403(b)s, which are designed for certain employees of public schools and state-run organizations; 401(a)s, not as standard, which are primarily for government and non-profit organization, 457(b)s, which are mainly for civil servants, municipal employees, law enforcement officers, and public safety personnel and profit-sharing plans.

They can also be personal retirement accounts such as Traditional Individual Retirement Accounts (IRAs) and Roth IRAs. The Traditional IRA is not taxed when you deposit the money, but when it comes time to withdraw the funds, you'll pay the taxes due at your income tax rate. A Roth IRA is taxed before you deposit it into the account, and the money is usually tax-free when you withdraw the funds. Roth IRAs are an attractive financial savings vehicle because investors can contribute to them regardless of age and take advantage of tax-free income in retirement, with no required minimum distribution, unlike a traditional IRA, which requires distributions at age 73.

Business retirement accounts such as Simplified Employee Pension (SEP) allow employers to set aside money in retirement accounts for themselves and their employees.

Of course, we all wish we had Defined Benefit Plans, another name for pension plan(s). A defined benefit plan is a promise made by the employer to make regular contributions to a pool of money set aside to fund payments to eligible employees after they retire.

All Assets Are Not Created Equal

A settlement might look like 50/50 on paper, but not in actuality. Here is a simplified example for conversational purposes only. One spouse will retain their 401(k) for $50,000, while the other will keep a Roth IRA for $50,000. The spouse with the 401(k) will eventually have to pay taxes on their future distribution (as it was deposited into the 401(k) with pre-tax dollars, say their tax rate is 20%, they will receive $40,000, while the spouse with the Roth IRA, already paid taxes on the deposited funds, will get the entire $50,000 in retirement.

Valuating and Dividing

The first step in dividing retirement accounts is to determine their value. Various methods exist depending upon the specific asset and state laws. Specifically, some qualified accounts can be distributed between spouses by utilizing a Qualified Domestic Relations Order (QDRO), a court order drafted by a QDRO specialist, allowing one spouse to roll funds over to another qualified account for the other spouse. Funds in Traditional IRAs, Roth IRAs, and SEPs can be transferred from the original account to another in the other spouse's name. Tax consequences may be incurred on specific retirement plans if a distribution is warranted. It is advisable to seek the assistance of a Certified Divorce Financial Analyst (CDFA) to ensure proper valuation and division of your retirement assets according to your unique circumstances, as each type has specific rules that must be followed and can provide personalized guidance based on your particular situation.

"Open the door...

it may lead you to someplace you never expected."

— Shu Uchida, a Japanese—Australian voice actress

13

Divorcing When You Are Older

A SECRET PASSAGEWAY

There is a growing trend sweeping the nation: Gray Divorce. Gray divorce is a term for divorce between older couples who have been married for a long time. This trend is gaining popularity as people live longer and reevaluate their relationships. According to Katie Couric Media, a 2021 report found that Baby Boomers got divorced at twice the rate of any other age group during the previous year.[1]

Ordinarily, long-term marriages are less likely to end in divorce, but couples over 50 are challenging this pattern. This movement tends to happen once the children are out of the house; the couple now has more time together and realizes they no longer have the things in common that they used to, or their goals no longer align. They may already live separate lives while still living in the same home. Thus, they are taking a step back to assess their relationship and begin a search for deeper meaning in their

---

1.

https://katiecouric.com/lifestyle/relationships/boomer-gray-divorce-increase/#:~:text=An%20April%202021%20report%20released%20by%20the%20U.S.,the%20rate%20of%20any%20other%20age%20group%20surveyed.

life. Their philosophy is to enjoy life to the fullest, as only one life is given. This leads them to a fresh start in their retirement years.

The thought of spending the next 20 or 30 years in an unfulfilling marriage prompts some to look for happiness elsewhere. Today, pursuing happiness and fulfillment at any age is more acceptable than in the past.

Financial independence, especially with women, has allowed women even to consider divorce, whereas before, they were stuck due to financially relying on their spouse or economic constraints. Advancements in careers and the ability to build significant retirement savings for themselves have empowered women to prioritize their happiness.

As we discussed in previous chapters, society has come a long way in the past few decades to make divorce less stigmatized. This has allowed older couples to divorce, something they may not have considered earlier in their relationship.

Economic Entrances

Divorce at any age involves the unraveling of a life intertwined. However, "gray divorces," which typically involve long-term marriages, present unique challenges. In these cases, the couple may struggle to distinguish their shared life from their own identities. They are intimately familiar with each other's habits, preferences, and possessions. Additionally, they may have accumulated significant assets such as retirement accounts, cash, and investments throughout their marriage. Splitting these assets can have far-reaching implications.

Moreover, economic consequences typically impact women more significantly, as they tend to earn less than men. As a result, women often experience a more significant decrease in income and have fewer years until retirement, as well as less time to recover financially than younger women. Additionally, women tend to have a longer life expectancy than men, which means they face a challenge in building assets that will last throughout their extended lifespan. Mistakes in financial planning can be particularly costly, and there may not be adequate time to recover from them. Therefore, the key to financial stability after a gray divorce is meticulous planning to ensure a smooth transition into retirement years and the next chapter.

Reflection Points

- When did you notice the disconnection with your spouse?

- What can you do to make the best decisions for your future?

A CDFA® is your golden key to making a complex

financial situation more manageable and less stressful.

14

Working with a CDFA

THE GOLDEN KEY

W orking with a Certified Divorce Financial Analyst® (CDFA®) before, during, and beyond the challenging divorce process is a game changer. What does a CDFA® do? A CDFA specializes in the financial aspects of divorce. Those who have worked with a CDFA® express that they feel better prepared, have more clarity, and get the support they need while stepping over the threshold of divorce.

The best way to utilize a CDFA® is to contact them <u>before</u> you contact an attorney or mediator. They will help you get ready and support you in determining how to make your divorce more financially feasible. They can judge the merits of a settlement and how to best structure it. Even though significant wealth might spur someone to contact a CDFA®, they are even more valuable for someone without a mountain of assets, as they will ensure you make the most out of what you have.

What are the key advantages that are often found when working with a CDFA®:

- Assist in a fair division of marital assets.

- Evaluate and help you negotiate the division of assets, spousal, and child support.

- Provide a clear picture of your specific financial situation.

- Assess short- and long-term implications of various settlement options.

- Offer empathy and understanding.

- Aid in creating a budget and financial plan for life after divorce.

For the reasons stated, it is said that people who hire a CDFA® to support them during a divorce experience more favorable outcomes.

We have already established that divorce is a complex situation with significant financial implications. Most people mistakenly believe hiring an attorney is the only professional they need with them on their journey. While lawyers have expertise in family law and can help you understand the legal aspects of your situation, the goal does not usually address your unique emotional and strategic needs. Divorce attorneys focus on being your legal advocate and will inform you of what a judge may decide if your case goes to court. They focus on what you want rather than what is best for you. This makes it essential to seek guidance from a CDFA®.

My client, Jane, approached me after she had already begun the divorce process with an attorney. Initially, she believed her lawyer was sufficient. However, as the expenses continued to mount, she realized her attorney was adept at offering legal guidance, managing her case, and involving her when necessary. What she determined was that she needed someone to help her comprehend her requirements, make informed decisions, and devise a plan for a just and fair settlement. By hiring a CDFA®, she felt confident in her decision and was proud of herself for taking control of her divorce journey.

A CDFA® can help you navigate the process and ensure a fair and well-informed distribution of assets. They tailor their advice to your specific circumstances and situation, analyzing all the nitty-gritty details to help you comprehend the financial consequences of your decisions. They can help you develop realistic budgets for your next chapter, examine tax implications, determine viable alimony payments, understand complex child support calculations, and divide retirement funds. This leads to a more equitable divorce settlement, providing peace of mind that your settlement is financially feasible and that you are set up for success as you transition to your new chapter and lifestyle.

Working with a CDFA® provides valuable financial insights, empowers you to make informed choices, and eases the financial burden during a challenging life event like divorce.

Reflection Points

- How can you utilize a CDFA® in your divorce?

Schedule Chat Here

"Be wary of little expenses.

A small leak will sink a great ship."

— Warren Buffet

15

Embracing Your Finances

BUILD A STRONG DOORWAY

anaging your finances after divorce can be an eye-opening experience, even if you were the one who handled them while married. Do you remember the feeling of riding a bicycle on your own for the first time? The fear that surged through your veins! You may have wondered if you could even balance this on your own at first. You may have thought, "I'm not strong enough!" You may have even screamed to your parent or sibling, "Please don't let go!"

Anyone who knew me growing up may remember me riding the "slow bike" or flipping over my handlebars while I flew down the hill. Truthfully, I never was any good at riding a bike. My fears got in my way. After getting divorced, some people feel this way when they start managing their finances on their own. The sudden shift in financial responsibilities and lifestyle can leave you feeling like you are riding the "slow bike" or flipping over the handlebars and leaving you breathless.

Fear not, grasshopper! With a bit of planning and following some helpful tips, you can master your money and be on a new journey to financial freedom. This is your time to shine!

Unlock the Door to Financial Clarity

Let's first take a deep breath! You've made it to the other side. But, now what? Most clients that come to me say they do not understand finances. That's not a problem; there is no better time to learn than now. Looking at your finances after your divorce is the first step towards financial recovery. Think of me as the person who is holding onto your bike while you are starting to learn to ride it. We are going to construct you a new house—your financial house!

The first thing to do is take stock of what you own (your assets—savings, investments, property, etc.), what you owe (your liabilities—debts, loans, credit cards, etc.), how much money you earn each month (your income), and where it is going (your expenses).

If the ink on your divorce agreement is still wet, you can begin with the items awarded to you in the agreement. Your Certified Divorce Financial Analyst® may have even prepared a lovely spreadsheet.

This is not just a mundane door but the entrance to your financial freedom. It doesn't need to be pretty, and the size does not matter; what matters is that you do it! This is the door of opportunity opening to successful money management.

Navigate the Hallway of Budgeting

This may not be the sexiest thing you can be doing after your divorce, but believe me, making your budget your new BFF has its privileges!

I know; you probably just grimaced. Did she say "budget"? I am not doing that! Can I skip this step? Absolutely not! Budgeting is of the utmost importance. Most think budget is synonymous with deprivation, but it should not be. It should be synonymous with the word empowerment! Empowerment to make real choices for yourself and give you the confidence to move forward knowing where your money is going.

Whether you make $50,000 or $500,000 a year, budgeting helps prevent spending beyond your means, which can happen at every income level.

Start with the income and expenses you documented and then track them monthly. Yes, monthly! Track **everything**—every streaming service you have, every Amazon purchase, and every fancy latte you buy. Once you know where your money is going, you can identify ways to cut back. Maybe you don't need Apple TV for the only show you watch, or you FINALLY cancel that "Subscribe & Save" for the tenth bottle of shampoo you already have in the bathroom closet. Remember that every small saving adds up over time! As I said previously, what I don't want you to do is deprive yourself—just like a diet that lacks calories, it is not sustainable. If you enjoy those fancy lattes, maybe you just cut back from getting them every day and get them only two times a week. You might even find that you look forward to and appreciate them even more!

So, keep those doors closed to unnecessary spending and track that progress! You need traction to make budgeting successful; it usually takes at least three months to figure out a good cadence and get the hang of it. So don't be discouraged, and keep it going. Seeing those savings add up or the debt decrease can be incredibly motivating!

I am most amazed when my clients get the hang of their budget, start digging into their goals, and make real progress. When an unexpected car repair expense pops up, they have it covered, or the dishwasher fails, no problem. They handle it with ease and grace. This is when they learn that having a budget prepares them—not just for the purchases they want but, more importantly, for what they need.

Unlocking Prosperity

What does financial independence mean to you? Now that you are divorced, it means something different than in the past. Does it mean standing on your own financially without alimony or spousal support? Would you like to save for a house, or do you need a new car? You may have walked away with some debt you need to release. Also, I am sure after the divorce, a vacation sounds enticing! Short- and long-term goals can provide purpose, direction, and motivation. It's crucial to ensure that these goals are specific and time-bound. You can accomplish a short-term goal within three to six months, while a long-term goal may be something you aim to achieve within three to five years.

Clear goals will keep you on track and motivated, regardless of your thoughts. Write them down. Display them somewhere so you can see them every day. Most people are visual creatures, so having it on display keeps it in front of your mind and reminds you why you are making such an effort. A picture on the fridge or the bathroom mirror? I like to make a vision board every year and mix it up when new goals are added. They don't have to be large poster board size; you can just do something simple whenever you have a goal or want to change it up.

Another great motivator is to think of a way to celebrate once you reach your goal. For example, if your goal is to not eat out for three months, you can treat yourself to a nice dinner after you complete that period. Alternatively, if you have been eyeing a new pair of shoes, you can reward yourself with them once you reach your goal. Whatever it is, celebrate your milestones! Enjoy the journey to financial freedom!

Reflection Points

- What does financial independence mean to you?

- What are your goals? (Specific, Measurable, Achievable, Realistic, and Time-bound)

- Short-term (3 to 6 months)?

- Long-term (3 to 5 years)?

- What would you like to display on your vision board?

- How would you like to celebrate each accomplishment?

Which Door Should I Open First?

One of the first questions clients ask me is, where do I start? Should I start investing? Should I pay off my debt? Should I create an emergency fund? The answer is yes, yes, and yes!

A couple of things go hand in hand, and you should do them simultaneously. First, if you are in debt, stop using those credit cards. Those credit card companies are money makers. They charge obscene interest, and you are giving them your hard-earned money. You would be appalled if you were to sit down and calculate how much you are paying the credit card company for the gallon of milk you placed on your credit card six months ago. So, start spending within your means. This is where cash flow planning and budgeting come in handy. You are on the road to success since you have already started this process! Next, establish a small emergency fund of about $1,000. If anything happens outside your everyday spending, like you need new brakes on your car, you have some money set aside and don't need to use those stinkin' credit cards.

Now, if you work for a company that has a retirement savings plan (401(k), 403(b), or 457(b), etc.) and offers a match, DO IT! Put as much in so you can receive the match. This means that if they offer a 3% match, but you also must put 3% in, to get that match, put 3% in! If you are in debt, do not put any more than the 3%. This is free money! The most important thing to note is this investment vehicle makes compound interest! Compound interest means making money on your money. Compound interest accelerates the growth of your investment over time.

Paying Off Debt

The most important thing you can do is prioritize paying off your debt. The interest rates I mentioned are like anchors trying to sink your ship. I know it is brutal and demoralizing, but it is necessary to move yourself forward. You are not alone; many are in the same situation as you. I had to pull myself out of debt after my first marriage. It was hard, and some days, I felt like there was no way I could do it. My ex-husband left me in so much debt that it made me sad and lowered my already low self-esteem. I didn't have the self-confidence to think I could do it, but I did, and you can too!

There are many methods, but I like to use the snowball method with my clients. The snowball method is a tried-and-true debt reduction strategy whereby if you owe on multiple accounts, you pay off the smallest balance first while paying the minimum payment on all the rest of your accounts. If two accounts have similar amounts, start with the one with the highest interest rate. Once you pay off the most minor account, move to the following smallest account. I like this method because it motivates you to keep moving forward. That is the intent, right? To pay it all off? When clients feel they are making progress, it excites them and keeps them on the right track!

Start by listing all your account balances in ascending order with the corresponding minimum balance. Don't forget to include loans, car loans and leases, health care debt, and tax debt. Commit to paying the minimum balance on each account and determine how much extra you can pay to the smallest account balance each month. Keep paying the minimum payments, plus the extra to the smallest balance, until the most minor account is paid off. Rinse and repeat for the following most minor account. Keep it going until all accounts are paid off!

An example of the debt snowball method is shown below. In this example, the debtor has the following amounts of debt that they need to pay after the divorce is settled (the debt is listed with the smallest balance first, as recommended by the method):

Debt	Balance	Monthly Minimum
Credit Card A	$250	$25
Credit Card B	$500	$26
Car Payment	$2,500	$150
Personal Loan	$5,000	$200

The debtor has an additional $100/month to be devoted to debt repayment.

*For illustration, we will ignore any accrued interest on each debt for the month.

The additional $100 is first directed toward Card A and, together with the $25 minimum payment, pays off the balance in two months. This is illustrated in the following table, with the prioritized debt indicated in bold and green.

Month	Card A	Card B	Car Payment	Personal Loan
0	**$250**	$500	$2,500	$5,000
1	**$125**	$474	$2,350	$4,800
2	**$0**	$448	$2,200	$4,600

Paying off Card A will free up $125 for additional payment: the original $100 plus the $25 previously committed to minimum payments on Card A. This amount is added to Card B's $26 minimum payment, paying it off in three more months.

Month	Card B	Car Payment	Personal Loan
2	**$448**	$2,200	$4,600
3	**$297**	$2,050	$4,400
4	**$146**	$1,900	$4,200
5	**0**	$1,750	$4,000

A total of $151 is then free for additional payment (Original $100 plus the $25 previously committed to minimum payments on Card A and $26 previously committed to minimum payments on Card B) and is applied to the car loan for a total monthly car payment of $301. This pays off the car loan in another six months.

Month	Car Payment	Personal Loan
5	$1,750	$4,000
6	$1,449	$3,800
7	$1,148	$3,600
8	$847	$3,400
9	$546	$3,200
10	$245	$3,000
11	$0	$2,800

The available $301 would then be added to the personal loan's minimum payment for a total payment of $501. This would pay off the personal loan in another six months.

Month	Personal Loan
11	$2,800
12	$2,299
13	$1,798
14	$1,297
15	$796
16	$295
17	$0

This leaves the debtor debt-free after 17 months. Every dollar put towards debt repayment is one step closer to financial independence. Each time you pay off a debt, it will feel like a weight lifted off your shoulders. Oh, what a relief it is! You will feel so much lighter and freer getting your debt paid off.

For me, snowballing my debt was a learning experience. I got acquainted with my debt—just like gaining weight is easy, but losing it is hard. Along the way, I was able to build new habits, such as having only one credit card, spending only what I could afford on it, and paying it off every month. Going through this taught me that I never want to end up in the same situation again if I can help it.

I am sure, whatever you do, YOU won't want to rack up debt again.

Establish an Emergency Fund

You need to be ready when life throws you a curve ball! As I am sure you are fully aware, things happen, such as needing new tires on your car, having an unexpected medical emergency, or having a job loss! Having an emergency fund can be a lifesaver!

The money you spent paying off your debt should now be used to build an emergency fund! How much should you save? At least three to six months of income!

This money is not for spending but for your peace of mind. If any unexpected circumstance arises, you have the money to pay for it without accumulating debt!

Savings and Investing

Once you have a handle on budgeting, your debt is paid off, and you have a significant emergency fund in place, the fun can begin. Investing! The goal is to start small, and once you become more comfortable, you can increase your investment goals! This is also the time to improve your 401(k) contribution. A Roth IRA is a great investment vehicle for your future. Drink it all in and learn as much as you can. The more you know, the more comfortable you will feel about investing and want to do it more!

Avoid Common Money Mistakes

Some of the most common money mistakes after divorce are overspending, neglecting retirement savings, failing to create a budget, and sticking with it! Don't let your emotions get the best of you and start to dictate your spending habits. Retail therapy can make you feel good ... temporarily! But once that Visa bill comes in, the heartache is right back. This can severely derail your financial recovery. Every dollar you can save is a dollar to invest in your future! Future vacations, future retirement, and future happiness! Many people have built a successful future after divorce, and you can too!

Seek Support

If you need someone to hold onto your bike while you feel more comfortable getting it on the road, help is here! I want you to succeed! There are many resources, from financial recovery coaches to support groups, for encouragement and guidance. They will help you become successful at money management after divorce. Remember, you are not alone!

Schedule Chat Here

"The wise man sees in every misfortune,

an opportunity for improvement."

— Seneca

16

Caring for Your New Chapter

PROTECT YOUR CHAMBER

Now that the ink has dried on your divorce document, you should do some essential things. Don't wait, don't pass, go, don't collect $200. At the moment, you may feel like there are so many other priorities that these tasks may seem minor, but neglecting them could cause problems later.

Change Your Passwords on Everything!

Yes, EVERYTHING! And I suggest doing this as soon as you know you are potentially going through a divorce. If they know your password, they will sign in to your accounts. Also, use a camera or bug detector to ensure no one is spying on you in your house or car.

We have all heard horror stories about exes getting into private files, reading emails, sliding into your DMs, or watching your every move. Protect yourself and change your passwords!

Cancel Those Joint Credit Cards

Let's face it: credit card companies are a big, lucrative business; they do not care about what your divorce agreement says, unfortunately. In their eyes, you are still responsible. Get that joint account PAID and CANCEL that card. You don't want something like this harming your future credit and making it difficult to get a loan or a mortgage.

One of my clients, May, who I worked with as a financial recovery coach, received her student loans and individual credit cards in the settlement, while her ex received their joint credit card debt. Her ex was responsible for taking her name off the joint credit card and paying it in full per the divorce agreement. However, despite his claims of contacting the credit card company to remove her name, he did not. He was late on payments, continued to use the card, and accumulated more debt. This not only affected May's credit score but also impacted her debt-to-equity ratio. She expressed regret over the situation and wished she could make different decisions, but unfortunately, there are no second chances regarding divorce agreements.

Make or Update Your Will and Beneficiaries

If you have a Will in place that was written with your ex, now is the time to get that refreshed. Maybe you no longer want to give all your worldly possessions to your ex, or you do not wish to be buried next to them. Along with the Will, make sure you include a Power of Attorney and Health Care Directives. Estate Planning documents can be morbid, but you must ensure your final wishes are understood and your loved ones are taken care of.

Does your 401(k) still have your ex listed as your beneficiary? You fought hard to keep your retirement plan during your divorce; don't let them get it if something happens to you! Beneficiaries trump those wills. So, RUN, don't walk, and update today.

Review Your Insurance Coverage

Your insurance needs may change after divorce! So, review your life, health, and disability insurance for your current needs.

You may need to find coverage if you were on your spouse's health insurance plan. Also, if you have anyone who depends on you, life and disability insurance is paramount.

Disability Insurance is the only kind that protects your income if you cannot work due to illness or an accident. Disability is something that we all feel can happen to someone else but not us! In 2023, the employment-population ratio for people with a disability was 22.5%.[1]

Your divorce settlement may or may not have had the criteria that you need to have a certain amount of life insurance to protect your children. God forbid anything happens to you! Your death would devastate them not only mentally and emotionally but financially, too! You are worth so much more, alive and kicking.

Hire a Financial Advisor and Coach

Now is the time to manage your own money your way. I support you getting your own financial advisor, not one you used with your spouse. You want someone who has your best interest at heart, not split loyalties. They will help you establish your goals and successfully lead you into your future.

I have a client, Jane, whose husband had a financial advisor who managed their money. She wasn't even invited to talk about their finances until she put her foot down once they started the divorce process. This advisor hadn't even met her, let alone get to know her or her goals. It is a critical time to have someone in your corner and to have your own goals to shoot for.

This is the new you. Hire a financial coach specializing in divorce recovery to help you move into the next chapter quickly and gracefully.

---

1. Persons with a Disability: Labor Force Characteristics - 2023 (http://bls.gov)

Hire a Divorce Recovery Coach

A divorce recovery coach assists individuals in creating new lives after divorce. They can help you heal, rebuild your self-esteem, and establish a fulfilling life post-divorce. Suppose you need clarification on the steps to take, are feeling stuck after a divorce, or are seeking out new friendships that understand what you are going through. In that case, a divorce recovery coach can guide you into this new chapter.

Learn more here:

"It's a beautiful thing when you choose to keep

going when there was a moment when

you were sure you would have quit."

— **Topher Kearby**

17

Moving On

WHEN ONE DOOR CLOSES, ANOTHER ONE OPENS

In life, we may encounter setbacks, loss, and an occasional disappointment (or two or three). However, these experiences may lead to new opportunities and paths we never expected. Life is unpredictable, but sometimes, the most valuable lessons can be found in unexpected places. While I was going through my divorce, a good friend told me, "Once you are on the other side, there will be many reminders of why you got divorced!" She was so right. Things that I didn't see or refused to see became clearer.

I eventually forgave myself for my struggles and moved forward. I understand now; I did my best with what I knew then. My side of the story doesn't matter anymore. It happened, it hurt, I healed.

For all those many nights I cried myself to sleep, I eventually mended. Well, truthfully, I still heal a little more every day. But I now appreciate why things didn't work out as I had hoped.

I am a member of a "club," one I hoped never to join but where members genuinely understand me and do not judge.

It is essential to take a moment to reflect on our journey and recognize our personal growth. Although we may face difficult times, we survive and usually become more self-confident. What we once thought was a misfortune is now seen as an opportunity for personal development.

There is still a battle within me, but I have changed. I am still a work in progress but no longer trying to destroy myself. Now, I am on a mission to save myself. I used to tolerate certain things but do not accept them now. When I used to remain quiet for fear of ridicule or criticism, I am now speaking up. I was once told I was too emotional, but now I wear the badge with honor. Yes, I am emotional; that makes me love hard, laugh often, and feel the world around me. I now understand my value and only give my energy and time to situations that deserve it. I look back at the person I was before my life was turned upside down and think of her fondly. I miss parts of her, but I am embracing the me I am now and who I was meant to become.

I yearned for an apology that never came. Instead, what I got was the outcome needed. One day, it finally hit me—it is no one else's job but mine to take care of myself. I realized that to move on, I had to be willing to let go. It is one of my most challenging life lessons. Change is never easy; you fight to hang on and let go. It is like being at a jungle gym and trying desperately to reach the other side. Your body is hanging, and your brain is trying to get your arms to move to the next rung, but you just can't muster up the strength—and you let go! Phew!

As a result, I closed the chapter of my old life, breathing a sigh of relief. This can take a bit, so be patient with yourself. A wise, influential woman always said, "This too shall pass." She is right; everything that hurts will eventually heal.

Here, I stand on the other side of the threshold. The closed door is behind me and serves as a reminder of my transformation from grief to growth. The uneasy feeling of change has faded, and I have carved a path to a new beginning. I am writing a new chapter. It is beautiful here, on the other side. The birds sing, the sun shines brightly, and I am stronger than ever. It is incredible how much you appreciate the small things in life after experiencing loss. To be alive, to breathe, to think, to enjoy, and to love. For the first time in a while, my soul feels free.

You are worth the struggle, the perseverance, and the determination. You have it in you, and you are not alone!

Journal Pages for Reflection Points

Workbook

Download your own workbook with valuable templates and checklists for your journey.

Access them through the QR Code below.

Get Workbook Here

Image Credits

Cover Open door by Anne-Marie Libotte from Getty Images

Chapter 1 Secret garden door by Gollykim from Getty Images Signature

Chapter 2 Strong wooden door by Martb from Getty Images

Chapter 3 Opened brown wooden french door Dmitry Zvolskiy from Pexels

Chapter 4 Three different color doors by YassminKa from Getty Images

Chapter 5 Open door to a green field by Photocreo

Chapter 6 Light escaping the room by Pexels from Pixabay

Chapter 7 Knock-Knock by Omayer Gharra from Getty Images

Chapter 8 Commercial building doors, steel doors by Aphisith Champalod

Chapter 9 Curious man entering in the book's door, fear of wisdom Francescoch from Getty Images

Chapter 10 Elevator by Empire331 from Getty Images

Chapter 11 Home key for unlocking the new house door by Shisuka

Chapter 12 House key in the door by Anawat_s from Getty Images

Chapter 13 Golden key by Orbon Alija from Getty Images Signature

Chapter 14 Hidden doorway by Teri Frisch from Getty Images

Chapter 15 Golden key is opening the door of success by Selimcan from Getty Images

Chapter 16 Vaulted Door by Altmodern from Getty Images Signature

Chapter 17 Lock your love by Triocean from Getty Images

Chapter 18 Open door by Peshkova from Getty Images

About the Author

S hell Sawyer, CDFA® is looking to change the way we speak about divorce. She believes that women have been made to feel like they don't deserve their share of the marital property. It is time to change the narrative. With the right tools, support, and mindset she feels we can do this together.

Shell is the Founder and CEO of Finding Strength with Shell based in Wethersfield, Connecticut. Shell helps women gain the strength and courage to get through their divorce successfully. As a personal divorce guide, mediator, and financial recovery coach, she helps you navigate the divorce process, make good decisions for your future, and move into your next chapter easily and gracefully.

Shell is a believer in lifelong learning. She holds a master's degree in accounting, is a Certified Divorce Financial Analyst®, a Certified Divorce Coach®, a trained mediator, and trained as a High Conflict Coach from Divorce Coach Academy. She also believes in giving back to her community. She is a member of the Board of Directors of Interval House in Hartford, Connecticut, a member of the Board of Directors for Greater Manchester Chamber of Commerce, on the Leadership Committee for eWomen Network Hartford Chapter, and a supporter of the Alzheimer's Association.

Shell lives at home with her fiancé, Scott, her dog Cypress, and two cats Layla and Lola. If you would like to learn more about Shell or schedule a consultation with her, please visit www.findingstrengthwithshell.com or scan the QR code below.

Learn about Shell

www.ingramcontent.com/pod-product-compliance
Lightning Source LLC
Chambersburg PA
CBHW060514130626
46553CB00002B/493